Three Wheels on the Wagon

Tony Fisher

Bon Voyage
Tony Fisher

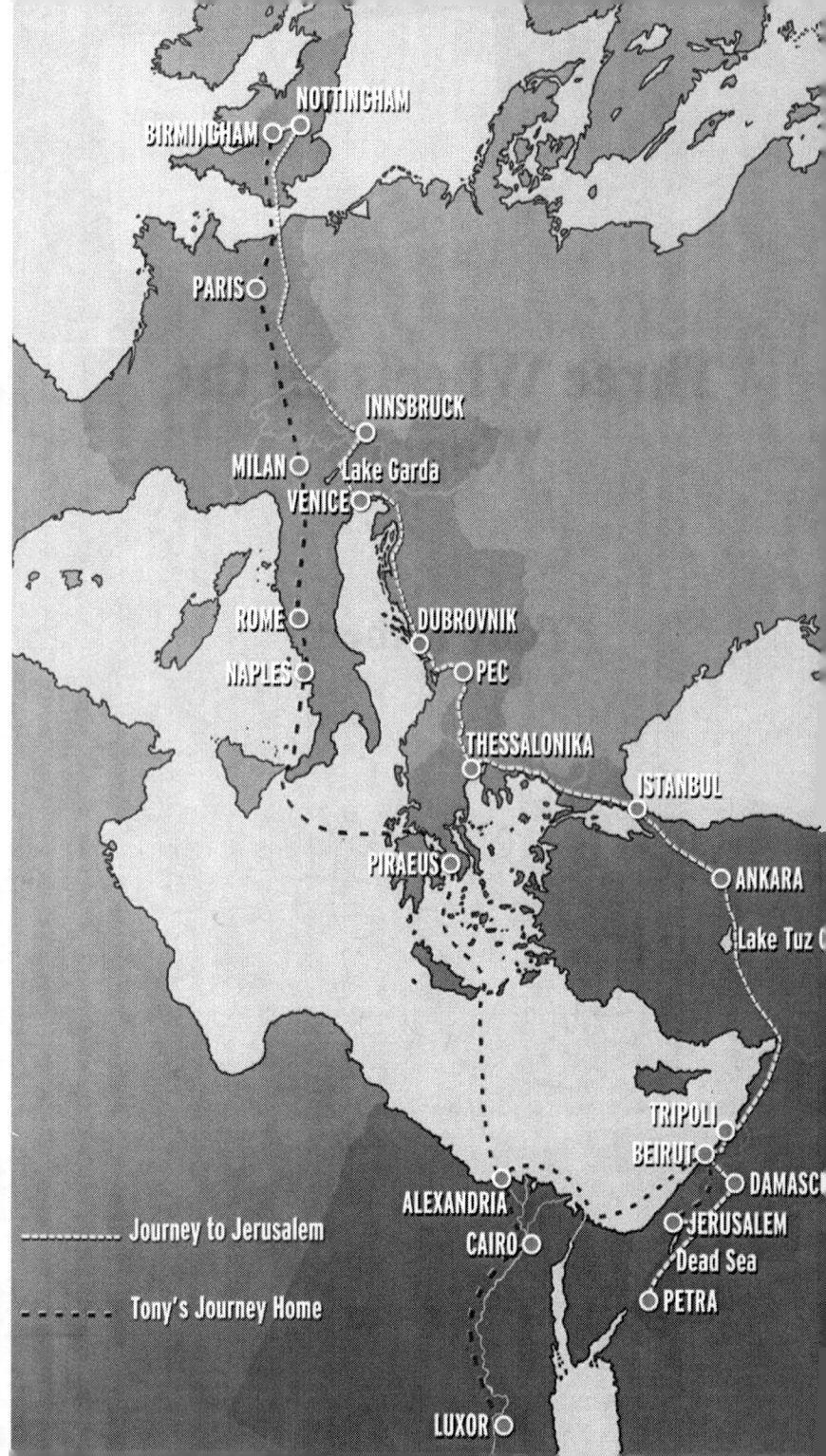

Published by New Generation Publishing in 2012

Copyright © Tony Fisher 2012

First Edition

The author asserts the moral right under the Copyright, Designs and Patents Act 1988 to be identified as the author of this work.

All Rights reserved. No part of this publication may be reproduced, stored in a retrieval system or transmitted, in any form or by any means without the prior consent of the author, nor be otherwise circulated in any form of binding or cover other than that which it is published and without a similar condition being imposed on the subsequent purchaser.

 New Generation **Publishing**

An RB Collection book

With thanks to all the members of the Great Mediterranean Circumnavigation Expedition.

And to all the friends and relatives who have kindly ploughed through these memories of the Sixties, especially Dave and Tina Archer.

But mostly a huge thank you to my favourite travelling companion: Camilla – this is why the housework and shopping were never done.

Preamble and Context

1966 was the year The Beatles released 'Revolver', the Moors Murderers were brought to trial and Evelyn Waugh died. But for most Englishmen it was the year we won the World Cup.

During a month of growing expectation and excitement, the home team battled its way nearer and nearer to the Final. Then the day itself: England versus Germany. The whole nation sat poised on the edge of its collective seats as two World Wars were replayed on one sunny August afternoon – in vivid colour at Wembley, and on flickering black and white screens across the rest of the country. Thirty-two million viewers, the biggest British TV audience of all time, held their breath, turning purple until the final whistle.

Three of us, however, missed the whole thing – barely realized it was happening. We had left the country weeks before the first ball of the tournament was kicked, long before Geoff Hurst scored that contentious third goal, or Bobby Moore raised the trophy to the roars of the entire country. When glasses were raised and tears of joy and relief were mopped from manly cheeks, we were a long way away, slightly puzzled as to why the Germans we'd met had suddenly become quite sniffy.

These are my recollections of the journey that we three absentees – Mike Jowett, Stephen Byrne and Tony Fisher – were on while the rest of the nation joined together, rejoicing in victory.

Forty years later, the three of us were together again, celebrating Mike and his wife Ruby's Wedding Anniversary. When we reminisced about our adventures that summer, the broad outlines were the same, but each of us inevitably had our own individual recollection of the details. And each remembered incidents the others had forgotten – or which had perhaps never happened. The re-telling and refining of anecdotes over forty years old, plus the fallibility of memory, takes its toll on absolute accuracy – the evolved stories can sometimes *become* the memory. So these reminiscences are written by someone looking through the wrong end of a telescope – at the caperings of three young strangers on another planet – and attempting to excise the myths that have grown in all our imaginations over all those years.

Fortunately, however, my old synapses are helped by an ancient archive: when my Mother died in 2008 and we cleared the family house in Northfield, I came across a thick brown envelope containing most of the letters and postcards that had been sent between my family, my girlfriend and myself while I was travelling. Having re-read them all, I then looked on my bookshelves for a stained and tattered copy of T. E. Lawrence's *Seven Pillars of Wisdom*, which had travelled with me. On a blank page near the back was a handwritten list of all the places visited on those travels. Finally, under the eaves in our attic, were a couple of boxes of faded 35mm slides taken on an old Ilford Sportsman and unseen for many years. What follows is therefore based on my memories, bolstered by these sources.

Unusually for a story set in the Sixties, it doesn't feature sex, drugs or rock'n'roll. Nor does it pretend to be a guidebook – on booksellers' shelves there are enough florid descriptions of Venice and walking tours of Jerusalem to make my efforts superfluous. This is simply a telling of our tale and the places and characters that we came across half a lifetime ago.

Mike and Steve were both twenty-two and just finishing a sandwich course in Building Management. I was twenty-one and starting my third job since leaving Moseley School of Art, working as a designer with Blomberg-Beaman – a small graphics company in Balsall Heath.

Mike came from Nottingham and had met Stephen when they began their course at the College of Advanced Technology. He was the antithesis of what red-haired people are reputedly like, being very sensible, quietly 'together' and able to think things through calmly and logically. A useful companion to have with you on a long journey or in a difficult spot. During the whole time we were travelling together, I can't remember him ever losing his temper or being stroppy, selfish or difficult.

A little time before we left to see a bit of the world, he became quite serious about a girl called Lois. She was part of a wider group of friends that often met at the 'La Boheme' Coffee Bar in Gosta Green. Her mother had recently died and she was left on her own in a flat at the top of a tower block in Perry Barr – not the smartest of Birmingham's suburbs. We were all sorry to know a friend was having a bad time, but Mike went out of his way to be particularly helpful and supportive. Then before you could say 'Let's take a trip around the Mediterranean', they were a proper couple – a significant item.

Lois must have had something to say about her new man preparing to disappear from her life for an unspecified time, but Mike typically didn't talk about their 'negotiations' to us. I suspect, after months of preparation, he felt committed to the journey and really wanted to go – and she was good enough to let it happen and trusted him to return in a decent state.

I can't remember, but I think they may have got engaged before we set off. And quite soon after he struggled back from the Middle East, they were married. Forty years, three children and numerous grandchildren later, they are still together.

Stephen Byrne was my oldest friend. We had shared a desk and formed a bond in our first year at the Oratory Secondary School in 1955. Initially, I liked him because he laughed at my jokes and awful impressions.

All the time I've known him, he has loved devising madcap schemes or ridiculous ventures, often designed to make lots of money, and always fraught with difficult problems. These would be solved in some sideways fashion that was puzzling but sometimes surprisingly effective. He would often become carried away with an overwhelming enthusiasm, which could be very contagious: he once convinced me that, if I jumped off the school roof holding a canvas camp bed above my head, I would swoop gracefully to the ground. I didn't. Later, he lost his eyebrows and most of his hairline in some gunpowder experiment that went wildly wrong

At the age of thirteen, he went off to Brooklyn Technical School and I passed for Moseley School of Art, but despite this our friendship survived.

He had had a turbulent childhood: his parents had separated and, in the early Fifties, Steve and his Father had left Dublin to come to England. When I first met him he was living in a local orphanage run by the Little Sisters of Charity. All the kids at the Oratory knew that they were neither little nor charitable. These ascetic Brides of Christ, with their nodding gull-wing hats, long gowns and clanking rosary beads, had taught me in junior school, so I knew they could be unyielding and stern. They all took the names of male saints – 'Sister Joseph' and 'Sister Vincent' – and in surrendering their female identity they seemed to have rejected warmth and approachability. They were scary creatures. It wasn't the best of environments for a young lad in his formative years, but, despite this, Steve always seemed easy-going and great fun.

A short time after our first meeting in the classroom, the Byrne family was reunited and Mr. Byrne became a caretaker in a series of state schools around the city centre. An empty school, in the holidays, or when all the staff and pupils had gone home, with all its equipment and huge echoing spaces, is a wonderful playground for two teenage boys. Plus the Byrnes were a boisterous, argumentative and eccentric bunch. Added to all those attractions was his sister Deirdre – a couple of years older than us, curvy and very aware of the effect she had on young men like me. The whole lot of them were irresistible, so I spent as much time in Steve's place as I did with my warm but very quiet Mom and Dad.

***

The journey that Mike, Steve and I planned together was a combination of The Grand Tour on a tight budget and a poverty-stricken pilgrimage. But, most importantly, it was an attempt at self-reliance and real independence. It was the sort of rite-of-passage that young men have always sought, but, in our case, without the need to put on khaki and kill foreigners. Most lads of our generation, if they were just a few months older than us, had done compulsory National Service. They were officially press-ganged and then exposed to the tough realities of the barrack block and even the skirmishes of Britain's dying Empire. We were very happy to have missed that, but we needed something to prove to ourselves that we could survive on our own, away from the nest. We were also part of the first generation of 'ordinary' working-class lads –

without a private income or rich parents – who could arrange sufficient time (in my case, by taking unpaid leave with a vague promise of a job when I got back), and scrape together just enough spare cash, to fund an adventure.

Mike had a smattering of schoolboy French, but none of us could be described as linguists. However, we were convinced, like generations of British travelers before us, that English spoken slowly and firmly, with a friendly grin and a bit of mime, would get us through most situations.

Uselessly, we did know a small amount of parrot-fashion Church-Latin, having all been brought up in a Roman Catholic/Irish tradition. Catholicism may, in fact, have been relevant to our choice of route: at least two of us had considerable reservations about our faith, so maybe this trip was an attempt to resolve our doubts one way or another. Perhaps visiting the source of Christianity would put everything in focus. It seemed to work for me – shortly after getting home I admitted to my parents and the Parish Priest to having mislaid 'the Gift of Faith'.

We were only away for a few months, but it was an interesting time in the Balkan countries, which were still welded together as Communist Jugoslavia under Tito. It was also a critical period in the Arab world, with all of Israel's neighbours threatening to invade and wipe it from the map at any moment.

The Jewish State was pictured in the British media at the time as a heroic David, threatened on all sides by powerful aggressors. And the next year, in '67, war with Syria, Lebanon, Jordan and Egypt broke out with catastrophic results for the Arabs, which we are still all living with forty years later.

Israel's Goliath days as the bully-boy of the Middle East, with nuclear weapons, land-grabbing, international assassinations, border walls and cultural apartheid, were some years in the future. At that time, most of us had considerable sympathy for the brave Zionists. The discovery of the concentration camps at the end of the Second World War made most Westerners of my generation sympathetic to the sufferings of European Jews, and we understood their desire for a homeland. We also knew from the media that they had taken unwanted, unregarded desert and made it bloom – there was little mention at the time that the land was already home to many Arab families, some of whom had been there for millennia.

Because all of the surrounding governments had closed their borders to the Jewish State, we knew we couldn't go into Israel and then be allowed into Egypt. A second passport was needed, plus a great deal of subterfuge to get back into any Arab country. But, to us, it wasn't very important. Almost all the significant sights of the Biblical Lands – for example, most of Jerusalem, all of Bethlehem, Hebron, Jericho, and a considerable portion of the Dead Sea, were then in Jordan. We must have been amongst the last travellers to see some of those places in Arab hands. So, if we were content to miss out on Nazareth and the Sea of Galilee, which were on the wrong side of the divide, Israel for us was just a logistical problem: how to get our motorbike and sidecar (if they got that far) around it and across the Eastern Mediterranean to North Africa.

***

We were travelling overland to the Middle East full of optimistic innocence, and without any of the props and professional advice available from today's tourist industry. Even guide and phrase books were scarce and seemed to have been written generations before, for gentlefolk on the Grand Tour or en route to the colonies. Stephen borrowed one for Jugoslavia from the library, which posed the vital Serbo-Croatian question: "Could you enquire of the concierge when my silver dancing slippers will be returned from the cobblers?"

And the only travel agency we were aware of was Thomas Cook, who dealt primarily with tickets for transatlantic crossings, cruises and first-class rail journeys. Not the wild schemes of impoverished youths. Flying anywhere was the privilege of the very wealthy, but there were the first glimmerings of the huge travel business that was to develop over the next three decades, with a few coach tours to the Swiss and Austrian Tyrol available to the reasonably adventurous. But, if you were young, poor and wanted to go somewhere for more than ten or fourteen days, you planned your own journey, bought the best vehicle you could afford and drove there, or got on a train, or hitch-hiked.

So, if we wanted to see the world, we had to start from scratch, learn as we went along and do it ourselves.

No wonder it was all a bit of a fiasco.

Tony Fisher, Birmingham, 2011

June 1966

ONE: *Goodbye and Good Luck*

The three of us stood and looked down at the sidecar. It was slumped under its mound of baggage and leaning against the kerb. We knew we had to get rid of a lot of this stuff, but we couldn't skulk back into the school and face all those people.

Stephen's Dad was the caretaker at King Edward's Grammar School just across the Five Ways Roundabout, and that Sunday morning the three of us had just revved away through the playground gate, followed by cheers and thrown kisses from a sizeable group of relations, girlfriends and well-wishers. They all thought we'd disappeared over the horizon, off on a life-changing journey through Europe and the Balkans to the Holy Land, then, if all went well, completely circling the Mediterranean: across Egypt, North Africa and finally back up through Spain and France.

They knew we'd be away for months and were missing us already. The tears were fresh in their eyes and their hankies still damp. So the idea of us chugging back through the gates within five minutes was unthinkable.

But even before I squeezed into the sidecar seat that morning, the luggage was almost completely hiding the bodywork and weighing down on its suspension. A couple of our friends mentioned that we looked a little over laden, but we'd assured them confidently that all this equipment was essential for the sort of journey we'd planned.

In truth it had all been collected over the previous months on the grounds that 'it might come in useful' or, more likely, just looked cool. We'd never loaded it all up before. So when it had been jammed into the sidecar – following a farewell party, at about 1am that morning – alcohol must have lent us a degree of misguided optimism. But now, having travelled five-hundred sober yards, with the tyre rubbing on the inside of the mudguard, we studied our packing a bit more critically.

Perhaps a full five-gallon jerry can of water wasn't really necessary, despite looking tremendously military and stylish. It was full of Birmingham water which was, we knew, the best in the world, whilst all foreign water was poisonous. However, the desert was a fair distance away and liquid weighed a lot.

We also came to the unwilling conclusion that an entrenching tool, an axe and 30ft of coiled rope, all slung theatrically on the outside, were probably set-dressing. And inside the stowage compartments we knew there were many other things that were less than essential – bought for their style rather than their usefulness. I think we imagined that we were latter-day Desert Rats battling our way to Tobruk through sand and bullets, accompanied by the theme music from the recently-released film *Lawrence of Arabia*.

But where to get rid of all the surplus stuff? It couldn't just be abandoned there in Calthorpe Road. We were too well brought up for that. So we decided to drive to my Mom and Dad's house in Northfield, about eight miles away, and offload our more imaginative items there.

My parents, meanwhile, had said their goodbyes to everyone at the school, walked to the bus stop and were also heading home on the No.22.

This bus route served much of the south of the city. It meandered through Edgbaston, Harborne and Weoley Castle before dropping them within a tidy walk of Black Haynes Road – a journey of at least fifty minutes. Despite this, Mom and Dad were settled at home and well into their first cup of tea before we surprised them by grinding to a halt outside. The bike was travelling very slowly under its load and we had managed to lose our way around our own city – not a good portent for the long trip ahead.

Following some serious thought and stringent thinning of the equipment – plus a cup of tea and some sandwiches – we said goodbye again and set off towards our destiny. Or, more precisely, north to Nottingham…Michael needed to say goodbye to his folks, and we were also going to meet up with the other members of the Great Mediterranean Circumnavigation Expedition.

TWO: *North, then South*

Despite getting rid of a lot of weighty stuff, the journey north was slow. Even on the M1, which had no speed limits in those days, the bike would slog along at about 40mph. This was because it wasn't in great condition.

Our Ariel VB had been built at Grange Road, Selly Oak, in 1956 and we had bought it a few months before from King's Motorcycles in the Horsefair for £59.19s.0d. It had a good number plate: TOF 80, but otherwise it wasn't a stylish or glamorous bike. I never really enjoyed the 'look' of it, with its clumsy cowling around the headlight, an ugly badge featuring a deformed horse's head, and the name 'Ariel' in a dull and stolid sans-serif. None of the swashes, swirls and vintage charm of 'Royal Enfield' or 'Velocette' – just a simple, unimaginative bit of type.

But the salesman at King's assured us that, with its single cylinder 600cc.engine, it was made to pull a sidecar stuffed with youthful dreams and unnecessary baggage – a solid, slogging workhorse that would drive us anywhere and everywhere without missing a beat.

He hadn't taken into account our mechanical inexperience and ineptitude.

It was the first motorbike any of us had owned, so we were starting from scratch. And we had no useful adults to help us, because none of our fathers drove, owned or knew anything about vehicles. My Dad taught me some calligraphy and the basics of drawing but would have been flummoxed if I'd asked him to explain how a clutch mechanism worked. Likewise, neither of the other two had grown up with elders who cleaned spark plugs at the kitchen table, or discussed gear ratios over a pint. Despite this, we became reasonably competent at basic running repairs, but would never have described ourselves as gifted engineers. Michael approached mechanical problems with a stoic, persistent logic; Stephen tended towards wild leaps of intuition that were either barmy or inspired; and I was happy to pass the spanners and offer slightly apologetic suggestions from over their shoulders.

We did make some very eccentric decisions. For example, soon after buying the bike, we took off the fuel tank, which was finished in standard Ariel burgundy, and re-sprayed it white, supposedly to prevent the fierce desert sun from evaporating or, worse still, igniting the petrol inside. An odd thing to do, but at least, when it was re-assembled, I was able to make sure the nasty 'Ariel badge was never replaced.

TOF 80 came fitted with a sidecar, which was just a large black box, probably designed for an itinerant workman to keep his tools in as he drove from job to job. We cut a hole in the lid and fitted a seat inside, so that only the passenger's head was visible. It soon became known to friends as 'the flying coffin', probably because they suspected that, if it stopped suddenly, the occupant would be decapitated on the raw edge of the opening we had sawn out, leaving the rest of his remains in the box, ready for a speedy internment.

We soon replaced it with a much more stylish sidecar, made with fiberglass which, we thought, bore some resemblance to the Second World War German Army model. It even had a rail in front of the seat, suitable for the mounting of a light machine gun – an item that never appeared for sale at our local Army & Navy Store.

The bike had probably already had a hard life, but, at first, ran quite well. However, on an early trial run out to the Malvern Hills, the oil feed blocked, the engine overheated and the whole thing seized. We ended up pushing it much of the way home and it was never quite the same again. Serious, proper men would have completely dismantled the engine, had the cylinder re-bored and fitted a new piston, but we had neither the money nor the mechanical ability. Our chosen alternative was to trust our luck and Brummy manufacturing.

Thereafter it was always difficult to kick-start, and quite often the engine would cut out and refuse to co-operate until it had had a little rest. It let Stephen down during his driving test. He was told by the examiner to drive around the block, whilst the man got ready to leap out into the road and test his emergency stopping technique. Who knows how long the poor bloke waited to pounce from behind a tree on Yardley Wood Road, because Stephen never re-appeared – the bike having had a seizure around some other corner. There wasn't time to arrange a re-take, so he set off across the Continent without a license.

Most of our other documentation wasn't very impressive. We had no repatriation, medical or foreign driving insurance, but we did all have imperious blue-covered British Passports, with the splendid opening page in fine English Roundhand, telling all foreigners to cause us no hindrance, on pain of the displeasure of Her Majesty's Government. Seemed enough to guarantee our safety and well-being anywhere, and each passport was satisfyingly stuffed with imposing visas for all the countries from Jugoslavia to Egypt, collected from their Consulates over the previous few months.

We had also bought an AA policy that covered us for the shipping out of spares in case of vehicle breakdown. And the AA supplied us with route guides, which listed directions such as: "leave the outskirts of

Damascus, passing a Mosque on the left and a telephone kiosk on the right; count seven telegraph poles then fork off along a desert track. Head towards the tallest of the distant mountains..." We didn't use them much for navigation, but they came in useful as lavatory paper in the moments of distress to come. Our safety equipment was equally impressive: one old, split cork crash helmet and two plastic builder's safety helmets 'borrowed' from a building site that Steve and Mike had done industrial release on. Like all similar helmets, they had no chin straps; they just balanced on top of the workman's head. But it didn't matter much; we only wore them if it rained.

Some time before leaving England, we took the Ariel to Vale-Onslow, a long-established motorbike spares shop on Stratford Road, and, in passing, told one of the mechanics where we were hoping to go on it. He kick-started it, listened for a moment, and then bet us a ten-shilling note that it wouldn't make Coventry, let alone Jerusalem. Months later we sent him a postcard from Istanbul suggesting he should pay up, but as the machine didn't last more than a few hundred further miles, I never went back to collect – perhaps one of the others did.

Eventually, the bike got to Mike's family home in the outskirts of Nottingham. They lived in a postwar prefab, very crisp and neat inside, and Mike's Mum made us tea and piles of sandwiches. I think all of our female relations were worried that we wouldn't get much food in the foreseeable future.

Later that day, the rest of the expedition turned up and Steve and I met them all for the first time. Firstly, Pat and Roger on a stylish Matchless 500 with chromed tank and a big Watsonian sidecar. Pat was Mike's younger brother and Roger his tall and funny best mate. Despite their relative youth (being two or three years younger than us), they had an air of competence and resourcefulness, which was confirmed a couple of years later when they drove an old ambulance overland to Australia. At that first meeting I knew, instinctively, that they were going to be good people to travel with.

The final members of the Expeditionary Force seemed a less impressive duo. Chris and Paul were slightly awkward, geeky lads who arrived in an old sit-up-and-beg Ford Prefect with its back seats removed to make way for their luggage. Paul couldn't drive at all, and Chris hadn't yet passed his test, so he drove, until he reached France, on 'L' plates, with his equally-unlicensed colleague pretending to be his legal chaperone. After Calais, they reckoned a licence, British or otherwise, didn't matter anyway.

I think all the Nottingham contingent had been Boy Scouts together, then, some years later, when Pat and Roger met the other two in a pub and told them about their intended journey around the Med, Chris and Paul whispered together for a moment, and then said they'd like to tag along. They made a spontaneous decision and everyone else unquestioningly accepted it.

There are many stories of Victorian and Edwardian expedition organisers spending weeks interviewing their potential team members, carefully assessing their various characters, qualifications and which school they had been to, but our little group of state-educated yokels seemed to have just wished itself together – without an organiser, and without us even meeting each other until the eve of departure.

Chris and Paul had only heard about the journey a couple of weeks before, so their level of unpreparedness was magnificent even by our slapdash standards. Their passports had no visas for any of the countries we hoped to visit, but they were blissfully unconcerned: "Don't worry, with a bit of luck we'll pick 'em up at the borders".

Steve and I shook hands with them and said hello. But inwardly I wasn't sure. I thought they lowered the tone a bit – spoilt my mental image of two magnificent motorcycle outfits surging across distant landscapes like a brace of racehorses, but were now tailed by that lumpy old donkey of a Ford Prefect. Fortunately I kept my snobby views to myself – if I'd voiced them they could have been flung back at me many miles down the road, because, as it turned out, their philosophy of trusting to luck and blind optimism worked extremely well: they got considerably further in their vehicle than we did in ours. Many, many weeks later, while we were standing at the sides of various Middle Eastern roads with our thumbs out, they were still motoring on in their unlicensed and unglamorous glory. So much for stylishness.

Looking back through the myopic mists of almost fifty years, reading my old letters and looking at the slides, Chris and Paul seem to have been bit players in my recollections of the journey. They and their car have a shadowy quality – a drive-on, drive-away part. After that initial meeting, we occasionally travelled in convoy, sometimes camped with them, and ate some meals together. I can recall rocking the black Ford to-and-fro when it was stuck on top of a rock on a mountain road, but I can't remember ever having a long conversation with either of them and they barely appear in any of the photographs – just peripheral figures on the edges of frame. They were certainly with us in Jordan when we all parted company and began to make our separate ways home...and then, as suddenly as they'd arrived, they disappeared from my life completely.

But on that first night, around the Jowett's table, we all seemed to get on very well. We talked and laughed together excitedly about the journey to come and then settled down to sleep, spread across the armchairs and floor of the living room. Just after dawn, Mrs. Jowett brought in tea and insisted we get up and join her at the parish church. She had arranged for a very early Mass to be said 'to ensure the preservation of our souls'.

Then, after yet more of her food, we finally turned south for Dover and the Continent, feeling very full and excessively blessed.

THREE: *Across Europe*

The annoying habit Europeans have of driving on the wrong side of the road was a problem for a motorbike with its sidecar fitted in the British style, on the left. Most of the time it was unimportant, as our limited speed meant that we were easily overtaken. However, on the rare occasions when we drove behind something travelling slower than us, like a hearse, a heavily laden lorry or a tractor towing a trailer full of farm workers, the person in the sidecar had to be nudged out into the oncoming traffic to see if it was safe to overtake.

"Outabit...outabit...outabit...GO!"

Or "NOOOO! GETBACK" if anything was thundering towards us on the opposite carriageway.

So whoever was sitting in the sidecar had the safety of the whole outfit in their hands. Mike and I were very cautious – an almost empty, straight road was necessary before we would give the thumbs up. Stephen, on the other hand, tended to be a little more cavalier every time he sat in the judgment seat. His idea of a reasonable gap in the oncoming traffic was a lot less comfortable than anything we would contemplate. When he shouted "GO", whoever was driving would drop down a gear, yank the accelerator and heave the bike as fast as it would go across the centre line of the road, often to be confronted by juggernauts or speeding cars blowing their horns at the idiots who suddenly appeared in their path. He would then giggle and shrug.

So whenever it was his turn to sit in the comfy seat and be the arbiter of our future, we became increasingly nervous. Eventually my desire not to have him and, much more importantly, the sidecar and luggage ripped from its fittings, resulted in us having a shoving and shouting standup row in the middle of a major road after a very close call with a speeding ambulance.

Like most arguments on the journey, it didn't resolve anything, but it made us both feel better. Spats happened from time to time, but sitting in such close proximity to two other people made sulking or holding grudges silly and pointless. It was also impossible not to be infected with each other's optimism: we were young, as free as we were ever likely to be, and, of course, immortal, so bad feelings mostly blew away in the slipstream.

The weather in France didn't reflect our sunny dispositions. A persistent raincloud followed us across most of the country, so the 'crash helmets' came into their own as hats. Later, when it got consistently dry and hot, they were only ever used as containers to siphon petrol into. In these early days of the journey, the three vehicles travelled as a loose convoy, each at their own speed, but meeting for a midday snack by the side of the road, often camping together and sometimes coinciding at petrol stops, where we were outraged at the price of Continental fuel: seven shillings and sixpence a gallon, or about sixteen and a half pence a litre.

Until it ran out, we mostly fed off food brought with us from home, bolstered by local bread, eggs and milk. And the evening meal was cooked on a tiny stove with a single burner, which worked off petrol from the bike's fuel tanks.

One typical 'Recipe for Seven Hungry Travellers' had a beefy theme:

1 packet of Vesta dried beef curry; 1 tin of corned beef; 2 packets of dried oxtail soup and 2 eggs. Add water, stir and then cook until the base of the saucepan is thick with coagulated carbon. Serve what is spoonable, accompanied by torn chunks of fresh bread.

The rain eventually stopped during our very short crossing of Germany, just a dash, past the town of Freiburg, to the Swiss border near Lake Konstanz. The Alps were bathed in sunshine and, with no shade on the bike, we all began to lose our city pallor; our Anglo-Celtic freckles ripened. Steve's face and arms turned beige; Mike's vivid pink; and I turned the colour of boiled gammon.

Despite our multicoloured magnificence, Switzerland was not pleased to see us. We met up with the others and camped in an unauthorized spot, inadvertently flattening some fine, tall Swiss grass. As we were beginning to cook a meal, a (Grass?) Warden puttered up on a small moped. He was incandescent, pointing furiously at the botanical tragedy we were causing. At first he threatened to fetch the police, but then decided that he would personally cast us out of his country. We hurriedly threw everything back in the vehicles and followed behind him for a couple of miles to the Austrian border. There he asked for our passports, made notes of all our names, then told us not to hurry back to his, now badly damaged, country. Perhaps the seven of us are still in some ledger of undesirables in a government archive in Geneva. I've never been back.

Austria, by comparison, was untroubled, even unmoved, by our visit and we spent a pleasant few days in a Youth Hostel in Innsbruck. As soon as we were settled, we all visited the Poste Restante Office to collect our mail.

In a time before most houses had their own phone, and neither mobiles nor email were even imagined, this was the simplest and cheapest way of keeping in touch with home. Letters from parents and girlfriends could be collected, on production of our passports, from the

PR counter at the main post office in most cities. The system operated everywhere, so we had arranged for letter drops at Innsbruck, Istanbul, Damascus and Jerusalem. Thereafter we didn't know what might happen.

The letters from my folks and Janet, my girlfriend at the time, are still delightful and full of interesting details about life in the UK in the 1960s: a holiday in Eastbourne; a shopping trip to town with Auntie Elsie; how the Football World Cup was going; how cousin David was doing in his first job at the Municipal Bank; what was happening in Janet's first year as a teacher...

By comparison, some of my letters and postcards are a bit embarrassing. The ones describing our life on the bike and daily routines are fine: straightforward and simple. But, alongside this, I was seeing wonderful things and couldn't help describing them in the most painfully stilted, bad-guidebook phrases. Although this purple prose is excruciating, perhaps coming from ugly old Brum was some slight excuse for all the over-expressed enthusiasm.

Since its beginnings in the Industrial Revolution, Birmingham was never known for its elegance. As an inhabitant once said in the 1850s, "It might be alright when its done'n'finished". And, by the 1960s, following the efforts of the Luftwaffe and then the town planners, it was very grim and at its most undone and unfinished. Almost all of the fine Victorian buildings that remained were black with grime and about to be demolished to make way for the new Car City, with its concrete tower blocks and pedestrian burrows. So it was easy for us to be impressed by towns that had encouraged generations of architects and masons to put up fine buildings, and then preserve them, just because they respected the efforts of their forebears and it made them feel good about their own lives and proud of their environment. A novelty for a postwar Brummie.

Perhaps in response to all this civic pride, we decided it was time to improve the looks of our own little outfit. Up until then our sidecar was patchy grey and white. So from a hardware store on the outskirts of Innsbruck, we bought tins of enamel paint, some good brushes, and then I got to work. I might not have been much of a mechanic but I knew how to hold a signwriter's stick, and soon the front hatch cover was emblazoned with a Union Jack and along the side ran the legend 'Birmingham to Jerusalem'. Below that were some Russian Cyrillic symbols which we believed read phonetically as 'succeed or bust' (unfortunately we never met a Soviet citizen to confirm our theory). The whole image was then framed by flickering flames. We thought it looked pretty stylish. When none of our fellow Hostellers actually laughed out loud at my efforts, we proudly kick-started TOF 80 and set off for the Brenner Pass and Northern Italy.

The rain caught up with us again on the evening we arrived at a huge, overcrowded campsite on the shore of Lake Garda. We were offered a tiny spot, right at the water's edge, and put up our tent on the granular, powdery sand.

Just as darkness fell the storm hit us. It poured down, and a vicious wind whipped away our pegs from their soft footings, bringing the sodden tent down on our heads. In such a raging squall it was pointless trying to re-erect it, so we scrambled out from under the soaking fabric, shoved it all under the sidecar and, with our sleeping bags tucked under our arms, ran in three different directions for shelter. I headed for the shower block, but then found that attempting to sleep, curled up on the duckboards of a recently used cubicle, while trying to keep a sleeping bag away from dripping walls, was hopeless, especially when the showerhead spluttered intermittently on my face. Eventually I gave up, and as the rain had stopped, I started to look for the others amongst the hundreds of dripping tents. It was the early hours before we miserably reconvened. Ah, the romance of the Italian Lakes.

At daybreak we looked and felt awful, but the rain had gone and the lake was in all its magnificent finery: water the colour of lapis, melting to a vivid emerald at the shore, then ochre rocks, orchards of lemon trees against a backdrop of grey-green pines, and finally the Dolomites reaching up to a perfectly blue sky. Enough, combined with a good Italian coffee, to raise a young chap's spirits and set him whistling on his way to Venice.

FOUR: *Venice and Dalmatia*

In Visconti's film *Death in Venice*, Ashenbach, the hero, arrives at the city on a small steamboat, dissolving out from a Turneresque pink and yellow mist, to the sounds of the Adagio from Mahler's Fifth Symphony.

Approaching on TOF 80 along a busy Autostrada, past the industrial horrors of the Mestre, across a rattling wooden causeway, then parking in a grey multi-storey, lacks some of that style. But catching a waterbus from that ugly concrete building into the Grand Canal, and seeing, for the first time, such a sweep of timeless, idiosyncratic elegance in every direction was like being hit in the back of the head by a sock filled with magic sand. The contrast between the utilitarian ordinariness of the parking bays and the miracle all around us was almost overwhelming. Surely nowhere could be this beautiful or ridiculously implausible. This exquisite place *really was* built on the waters of a lagoon. Even my sense of smell was zapped. One moment, the stink of petrol and dusty tarmac, the next a heady mix of hot, ancient stone, mildewed plaster and faintly fetid, salty water. Like thousands of other first-time visitors over the centuries, all three of us just stood and stared. We were impressed by Venice.

Even the hospital was enthralling. Stephen had developed an irritating rash on his hands, and as neither Mike nor I wanted to catch whatever he had, we encouraged him to go to out-patients at the Ospedale. Out of idle curiosity we went with him and sat in a breathtaking waiting room, looking up at a vaulted ceiling covered in seventeenth-century frescoes of angels and saints doing charitable things to poorly mortals. You didn't get that at Selly Oak A&E. This passed the time until Steve, our very own mortal, came out of the treatment room accompanied by an angelic creature that had obviously just popped down from the plasterwork and slipped into a shapely, white nurse's uniform in order to mop his brow. As they both crossed towards us, he was staring at her so fixedly that he threatened to walk over several items of furniture and small children. I think he felt that having itchy fingers was a small price to pay for her slightest attention. She told us, in broken English that made us all tingle, that the doctor thought it was probably a reaction to motor oil and he should avoid too much fiddling with the engine for a while. We both nodded with silly grins. We'd have smiled like that even if she'd told us it was terminal and that we should take him out and drown him in the canal.

Despite the almost irresistible beauty of Venice, eventually we hit the road again, east to Trieste then south along the Adriatic shores of Jugoslavia. It was high summer and getting very hot, but the empty road hugged the coast all the way and the warm sea was peppered with small islands, which broke up any swell and made it very calm. The day started with a swim before breakfast and we swam whenever the mood took us. There were often times on the journey when we were filthy, but for the whole length of Croatia our skin was spotless, wrinkly and almost waterlogged.

Pitching a tent was both difficult and pointless; there was no earth to drive pegs into and the rocks held the sun's warmth for hours after it had gone down. So, at night, we spread out our sleeping bags on the flattest boulders each of us could find and slept. It was hard on the back and hips, but made packing up the next morning very simple. However, by the time we got to Split, the idea of lying on a mattress for a couple of nights had become very appealing.

It seemed that Tito's Communism couldn't stop private enterprise entirely. Women were gathered in loose groups along the Split waterfront, offering various services to the sailors who landed there. Amongst them were older ladies who had rooms for rent. Using a combination of mime and Euro-speak, we struck a deal with one who indicated that she had three vacant beds, then she motioned for us to get back on our bike and follow her. She climbed into a battered Soviet pickup, driven by her hulking son, and roared off in a cloud of black smoke. After a choking ride following them to the furthest outskirts of town, we were shown into a tiny flat in which eight people lived a cramped existence. After a bit of whispering, grumbling and re-shuffling of all their accommodation, we were given a clean, bright room with two single beds and a mattress on the floor. Much nicer than rocks.

The next morning was Sunday, and Michael suggested that we go to Mass in the Cathedral at Diocletian's Palace. He was overheard by Madam's daughter, an intelligent, attractive girl in her mid-twenties who was home for the summer from Belgrade University. She spoke good English and proceeded to grill us, politely but firmly, as to why three *reasonably* intelligent young men would waste their time indulging in such ancient, outdated claptrap.

Just as we had all been inculcated with the habit of Catholicism since birth, her arguments came from a lifetime of strong state atheism. She was a new socialist woman: confident, sure of her opinion and didn't believe her lack of penis made her arguments less valid. A new and impressive sort of creature for Englishmen to come up against. It was a good discussion and, I think, the first time in my life that I had heard the case against God put well and persuasively by someone of my own generation. Not exactly an Atheist Epiphany, but her arguments rumbled unsettlingly around in my mind for a long time.

Down the rest of the long Dalmatian coast, we motored in convoy with the Matchless and the Ford. Our travelling developed a rhythm, where motion became an end in itself. The vehicles were going well and we just had to push on. There seemed less time to stand and stare, so we saw very little of the pretty towns along the shore. Even the lovely walled city of Dubrovnik didn't delay us for long. I had to go back many years later with my family to enjoy it properly.

This tendency of the long-distance traveller to just keep going, at the expense of what's on either side of the road, is a pattern we fell into occasionally on this trip. But something usually happened to break the rush and make us stop. This time it was Jugoslavia that brought us to an emphatic halt – at the Albanian border.

FIVE: *A long and winding road to Kosovo*

Albania's totalitarian ruler, Enva Hoxha, was not at home to visitors. The place was locked, barred and bolted to every outsider. It remained that way until the early 1990s, and when a few visitors began to trickle in, they found a barren, depressed country covered in small one-man pillboxes, tank traps and trenches, all waiting for an invasion or other threat that never materialized. No one wanted to invade that sad place.

In 1966 there was no way through Hoxha's paranoid republic, so we had to go around it. All seven of us sat down together on the shores of the enormous, dark Bay of Kotor and studied our maps. We had to go north to Titograd, the chief town of the Montenegro region, then turn east until we got into Kosovo and finally south through Macedonia towards Greece and Turkey – three sides of a square.

Our map showed that the main road took us many miles away from Albania before it finally turned in the direction we wanted to go. It would take forever to follow that big red line. Then someone pointed out another route that skirted very close to the Albanian border, which would save us miles and miles. True, it was only a squiggly little thing, across what looked like some big mountains, but a road is a road…isn't it?

Optimism and blissful ignorance took us to all sorts of wonderful places – it was what made us start the journey in the first place. But, occasionally, we came unstuck. The civil engineers that had built this path of good intentions had started off with a little jape: "let's tarmac the first seventy-five miles, just to lull travellers into thinking it's a good road, and then…"

When we reached the end of the smooth, black surface, we looked up to see that our route became a dusty, narrow path, pitted with big holes and strewn with boulders, winding very steeply up to some very imposing peaks. (Montenegro means 'Black Mountain' for a good reason). At first we were depressed. Then hope kicked in: "Perhaps it's just road-works, and there'll only be a few miles like this before it becomes tarmac again".

It wasn't. And it didn't. We pressed on, very slowly to avoid the worst of the potholes and rocks and stopping often to push and heave one of the vehicles out of a particularly bad hole or off a boulder. A cloud of thick, grey dust was spun upwards by tyres that couldn't get a grip on the increasing gradient. By the end of the first day, this blinding choking powder had penetrated every surface, orifice and crack on us and our vehicles so that we merged into the landscape. If they stood still for a moment, we couldn't tell where our friends began and the rocks ended. It was a tribute to the bikes and car that the filthy stuff hadn't penetrated the fuel lines or carburettors and ground us to a final halt.

In the fading light, we tried to dust ourselves down, in order to recognize who was talking, and then reviewed the situation. One option was to go back down that awful path until we reached the main road and then set off along the big red routes. That would've been quite sensible, but it felt rather defeatist. If, on the other hand, we went on, it was quite possible that the road ahead would become smooth and metalled very soon. And that ridge we glimpsed above us was almost certainly the summit of the pass between the mountains. Then it would be downhill all the way into Kosovo.

But as any walker will tell you: climb the ridge above you and another ridge is waiting. Climb that ridge…and so on.

Two soul-shaking, puncture-ridden days later – having seen almost no humans, other than a distant figure on a donkey and a few deserted hamlets – and after intense rainstorms and terrifying hairpin bends with sickening drops, we finally breasted that ultimate ridge and saw a straight, flat highway leading down to the small, Kosovan town of Pec. Few people would put this unpretentious little place in their 'top towns' list, but to us, with its paved roads, cafes, showers and beds, it wasn't just bricks and roof tiles, it was heaven with an Islamic touch. The skyline of this bit of paradise was decorated with a minaret and dome, rather than a church bell tower. We had reached the fringes of the old Ottoman Empire.

We often caused a bit of a stir when we rode into town, but the arrival of our three dust encrusted vehicles with their ghostly white passengers into the main street was greeted by wide-eyed stares from quite a crowd. One or two clapped and smiled, but most eyed us with considerable suspicion – we were very foreign, and we had come down from the mountains.

After a meal and a decent sleep, several hours were spent trying to rid ourselves and our machines of the Montenegrin mountain dust that was hidden everywhere, from our cooking pots to our noses and ears. Then we began to investigate what the last few days had done to the machines. The Ford had survived very well – just patches on the patches on the inner tubes, some alarming creaks from the suspension and a bent exhaust. The Matchless had to go into a local repair shop for some welding on cracked front forks. But the state of TOF 80 was more puzzling. Its innards were noisier and it was travelling even slower than before, but to our inexperienced eyes there was nothing noticeably wrong. In hindsight, that awful road had shaken it very badly and it was nearing the end of its useful life.

It was soon time to move on again and in Pristina the convoy split up – each vehicle to travel at its own speed. We arranged to meet up across the Greek frontier in Thessalonica sometime soon.

Our drive on TOF 80, down through Kosovo and Macedonia, was great: almost deserted, winding roads across beautiful rolling hills, with those big, dark mountains keeping a decent distance. Nonetheless, we were high enough for the weather to be unsettled – mostly hot sunshine, but broken by short, intense storms. One afternoon we were chugging along, dry and warm, while fifty yards to our left a long wall of rain started to fall on the fields from a single bank of black cloud. For minutes we drove alongside this sheet of water before it moved across us and we got a soaking.

Driving along on our slightly eccentric combination, we were usually regarded with interest, occasionally admiration, but almost always with humour and warmth. I don't know about the others, but, being a bit of a show-off, I liked the reactions we got. However, on one of those balmy Kosovan days, we became the centre of a small, angry storm. A long stretch of road was being dug up and the carriageway was reduced, by a series of poles and ropes, to the width of one vehicle. We were waved through by a man with a green flag and had gone about a mile down the narrow pathway, almost to the end of the works, when a local bus pulled onto the single lane and started down towards us. We met, nose to nose, and stopped. The bus driver furiously indicated that we should either back up or evaporate. We refused – we had neither a reverse gear nor the inclination to give in. So over the next ten minutes, a nasty row developed, each aggrieved party protesting loudly in a language the other didn't understand. The driver and some of his passengers got down from the bus and encircled us, poking us with their fingers and shouting in our faces. One woman even kicked the sidecar as we stood there, arms folded, stubbornly insisting that this wasn't fair; we had almost reached the end of the detour and should be allowed to continue.

There were an awful lot of them and only three of us, so I was beginning to feel we were well out of our depth, when, fortunately, the noise attracted the attention of the Civil Engineer and a gang of his navvies. Speaking both English and Serbian, and exhibiting admirable diplomatic skills, he quickly calmed the shouting, got all the passengers back on the bus and ordered his brawny bunch of men to simply pick up our motorbike and sidecar with all its luggage and gently carry the whole thing sideways, across the ropes and onto the dug-up roadway, until the bus had passed.

That way no blood was spilt and no one lost face. Unfortunately, several of the people on the bus couldn't resist spitting and swearing at us as they drove past, but the Engineer explained that they were just ignorant peasants who knew no better and we should try to forgive. I think we were quite glad not to be dangling from the three nearest trees, so were happy to agree. And I expect he'd told them that we were arrogant, oafish tourists, but nevertheless guests, and hoped they could find it in their hearts to understand us. But whatever had been said, it had sorted a potentially nasty bit of road rage admirably.

As we continued down through those lovely Balkan hills, our lives became increasingly simple and primitive, reflecting the wildness of the landscape. We went to bed when the daylight faded, then when the sunrise woke us up we washed ourselves and brushed our teeth in streams. We defecated behind bushes, wiping ourselves on the largest leaves available and burying the results. (That entrenching tool left back in Birmingham would have been useful after all). One afternoon, when squatting with my trousers around my ankles, I was startled by a loud rustling behind me. I leapt up, convinced that I was about to be lunch for some ravenous wolf or bear, but instead found a large, wild tortoise careering down the slope past me. Sudden fear and a diet of good Slavic fruit are remarkably effective laxatives.

Nights in the hills were colder than on the Dalmatian coast, and it would often rain. But fortunately there was good soil to drive pegs into, so it was worth putting up the tent. At the end of each day's driving, we preferred a camping spot well away from villages, in case we inadvertently trespassed onto someone's land. We wanted as desolate a spot as possible, amongst just the hills and forests with no houses or farms around. But one evening, camped in seemingly uninhabited isolation, we were just clearing up after a simple supper when we spotted the figure of a man tramping towards us. As he came nearer we could see he was wearing a battered felt hat, tight-legged, Turkish trousers with the crutch almost as low as his knees, and a big sheepskin cloak. Someone whispered that the Grass Warden had perhaps followed us from Switzerland. However, when he reached our tent, the man seemed delighted to see us. He shook our hands and smiled broadly from behind a big moustache. This was the farmer of the land we were on, and although he hadn't invited us, we were nevertheless his welcome guests. From beneath his sheepskins he produced a lidded earthenware bowl and presented it to us. It was filled with creamy-white yoghurt. Handshakes, bows and big grins again, then he turned and headed back the way he'd come.

In the 1960s, young men from a British working-class background had no experience of yoghurt and even less of the forms of politeness involved in a gift like this. Should we have just a small amount each and then return the rest, or would that be seen as a rude refusal? Was it the family's ration for an entire week or a basic everyday commodity? And why did it look so good, yet taste like something left at the back of Granny's cupboard for too long? In the end we decided to mix all of it with some precious jam we had bought in France, to soften its sourness and attempt to eat the lot. The agony of social niceties!

Sometime later, another, smaller figure tramped up to our camp. It was the Farmer's son, who looked about ten or twelve. He indicated that we should pick up the bowl and follow him. We reckoned that a reciprocal gift was called for, but couldn't think of what was suitable or what we could spare. Finally we grabbed a pack of Co-op tea and some sugar.

We hadn't seen the farmhouse because it was tucked away, down in a fold of hills, several hundred yards from the road. It was one storey and made of stone and clapboard. Outside a few chickens rooted about.

Inside was just one long, low room. A cooking fire was burning in a simple hearth. Nearby, on the earth floor, was a wooden plank table with simple, backless benches either side. Hanging on one wall was a framed, faded photo of a richly mustachioed elderly man, probably the grandfather of our host, and opposite it, a calendar showing a picture of a mosque. Rolls of bedding were piled in another corner.

Our host introduced us to his son, his wife and their two small daughters and then asked us to sit. We presented our gifts, but they were puzzled by the pack of tea. Without a common language and with the limitations of mime, it was impossible to describe how to make a cuppa, so we had to demonstrate. With the wife's permission, we boiled a pot of water on the fire, added a handful of tea leaves and stirred. When we poured it out into a clay beaker, we hadn't got a strainer, but we hoped that plenty of milk and sugar would make it drinkable. We hadn't got milk either, but this was a farm – there must be gallons of the stuff somewhere.

But how to describe milk in mime? Even three naive Brummies realized that most of the cultural icons relating to British milk wouldn't work in Kosovan terms, such as the jolly, whistling milkman delivering a daily pinta to the doorstep. And our little mimed drama of where milk came from biologically caused lots of laughter but no exact understanding. Then, in a moment of inspiration, one of the girls ran off and returned with…more yoghurt. The resulting awful drink was passed between our hosts. They all smiled politely and nodded approvingly while trying to pick the leaves out from between their teeth, except the youngest child who couldn't quite hide her disgust.

(Later, as we got nearer to Turkey, it dawned on us that they would have understood the concept of tea-drinking very well; sweet tea with a sprig of mint shoved into it was a ubiquitous drink in the old Ottoman Empire. The lack of mint, and our substitution of yoghurt, was the surprise element).

It was, however, a lovely evening. We laughed a lot and, despite the lack of a common tongue, learnt a surprising amount about our very different lives – but I don't think we gained much appreciation of each other's cuisine.

In the early hours of the next morning, we were woken by a high wind and pouring rain. A small stream of water ran through the tent, soaking Mike and Steve in their sleeping bags. I was nearest the flap but completely dry, so when the other two suggested I should go outside and check the guy ropes, I argued that that would make me as wet as they were. They didn't mind that. I did, and I refused point-blank to budge. Eventually, after a lot of quarrelling and grumbling, Mike clambered across me, making sure to knee me in as many soft places as possible, tightened the ropes, then returned sopping wet. He didn't respond graciously to me asking him not to drip all over my bit of the tent. Not our finest moment as a team – or mine as a member of it.

Our petty squabbles about trickles of water were put into perspective when, the next day, we drove into Skopje. Three years before, the city had suffered a major earthquake and evidence of it was still around, with crushed and mangled mounds where buildings had fallen in July '63. Many of the survivors were still living in temporary shelters, and the damage extended far beyond the city. All across the hillsides of the Vardar River Valley there were ruins of houses and farms and ugly cracks across the roads. A lot of people's lives had ended or been irreparably ruined in that short burst of vicious energy.

Shortly before leaving the Valley we arrived at the rear of a traffic jam. We hadn't been in one of those since leaving home. Mike was driving, so Steve and I strolled forward, rounded a corner and saw that the queue snaked down to a river and a military ferry, which had replaced a fallen bridge – the boat went slowly to-and-fro across the water, taking a few vehicles each time – and ahead of us was a very, very long line of traffic.

A smart, young Army Officer patrolling the queue stopped and looked at us and our outfit. We smiled. He didn't. He walked slowly around TOF 80, paused…and then pointed emphatically towards the river, looking for a moment like one of those heroic bronze statues that infest many town squares. "You go!" he barked.

Perhaps to the Jugoslav military mind, any motorbike was a narrow, two-wheeled vehicle that could be squeezed into a small space on a boat deck (even when it has a large lump of sidecar strapped to the side). Or perhaps, despite the serious expression, he was an Anglophile and approved of the Union Jack on the hatch cover. Or perhaps his Uncle owned an Ariel. Whatever the reason, we were ushered out of the line and, despite our assurance that, of all the people there that day, we had the least reason to push to the front, we were ordered down to the quayside and on to the ferry. We drove slowly past dozens and dozens of rather peeved motorists and could only shrug guiltily and do our "sorry...nothing to do with us, honest" expressions.

This sort of casual kindness and genuine hospitality, often from people whose life was, compared to ours, very hard, was typical of this dramatically lovely and welcoming country. Except for some of the road surfaces and the confrontation with the bus, we were sorry to leave it all behind at the frontier.

SIX: *Istanbul*

A Greek welcomed us on our first night in his country by stealing all our tools. We had camped on a beach east of Thessaloniki and prepared to work on the engine, which was needed badly because of misaligned timing gears. Adjusting the cogs and chain was becoming an increasingly regular chore, a symptom of a machine in decline. No doubt a well-equipped workshop with access to good spares could have pulled it around even then, but three amateurs at the roadside could only nurse the poor old thing along.

It was backfiring loudly as we arrived at the shore and although we thought the sweep of sand was completely deserted, our noisy entrance probably alerted someone to our presence. After resetting the cogs, but before we had time to fit the outer casing back on, the sun went down and plunged us into deep, dark night-time. There was no moon and we had no decent torches to carry on with, so, foolishly, before climbing into our sleeping bags, we left the toolbox tucked under the sidecar, intending to finish the job in the morning. When we woke, we'd had a nocturnal visitor, and the box, with its familiar collection of old, rusty spanners, tyre-levers and screwdrivers, had gone.

Losing the tools was bad for the bike and a knock to our confidence. Almost everyone we'd met so far across Europe and the Balkans had either ignored us and let us get on with our journey, or we'd been welcomed and treated with honesty, tolerance and generosity. This made us very relaxed, even careless about our belongings, and perhaps ourselves. Now a touch of uncertainty dawned...perhaps not everyone we met meant us well. We were certainly annoyed with the Greeks, blaming every native for the work of one little sneak-thief, and we adopted an instant, silly prejudice: we didn't like this country or trust its people and wouldn't be spending any of our money in Greek shops replacing our tools...so there! An easy promise to keep, as the chances of buying decent equipment along that stretch of the Greek coast with its tiny fishing villages were almost nil. The next real opportunity for buying anything more complicated than food would be in the markets of Istanbul.

The engine casing was screwed into place with the edge of a small coin and Mike's little penknife, and we set off across Northern Greece towards the Dardanelles in a subdued mood, crossing our fingers that the timing didn't slip again before we could buy a replacement tool kit.

Two days later we crossed into Turkey, travelling alongside the Matchless with Pat and Roger. It was July twenty-eighth and my twenty-second birthday, so we decided to raise our spirits with a slap-up double celebration: firstly, we had managed to avoid any other Greek tragedies, and secondly, I was now the same age as Steve and Mike.

Choice of party venue in that desolate strip of borderland was a bit limited: one ramshackle hut on the side of the highway, the local equivalent of a transport caff. It was indistinguishable from many other establishments we'd eaten in across the Balkans, and offered exactly the same menu: small grisly pieces of goat or mutton, grilled on a skewer over an open fire and wrapped in flat-bread, then served with some limp salad. They called it a kebab. There was no way of knowing then that this would one day be the favourite cuisine of the inebriated all over Britain.

But our celebrations didn't stop at just a kebab, because that night was a birthday party. We also had intensely sweet Suclat rice pudding followed by fresh peaches, pears and honeydew melon, all washed down with mint tea, beer and plenty of Arrack – an aniseed-tasting booze designed to give you the mother of all hangovers the next morning. The whole feast cost us five shillings and sixpence each (27p).

Some locals strolled in with a couple of lute-like instruments and a large, flat drum and played some songs. Pat got his guitar from the sidecar and we sang some of our songs back. The beer and the arrack flowed and we were soon all best friends. The English and Turks were princes amongst men, but Greeks were all tool-thieves and horse-bandits...another round please innkeeper.

I must at this point say sorry to all Greeks (except the one who pinched the toolbox). I have been back since and found them to be a welcoming, honest and charming people who have stolen nothing else from me, and I now have a great affection for their beautiful country. However, that night they acted as a bond between our new Turkish brothers and ourselves. We were linked by our common mistrust of someone else, and the power of bad singing.

The next morning, during our drive along the Sea of Marmara, none of us were feeling our best. Then, at midday, on a stretch of road without a scrap of shade, the Matchless had a puncture. This was quickly mended, but when Mike tried to kick-start our engine it refused to fire. He began to undo the engine covers and the whole clutch mechanism fell out into his hands – the threads of the bolts holding it together had worn away.

Whenever one of the machines had a problem, no matter how bleak and isolated the spot, a small group of locals would quickly appear from nowhere and stand around enjoying the free show. Fortunately for us, the crowd that gathered that day included a young lad who said, in halting English, that he could get it fixed. He said it so quietly and earnestly that we believed him and handed over the pieces of metal. We had nothing to lose – without a clutch we weren't going anywhere.

He climbed onto a small two-stroke bike and buzzed off along a dirt track toward some low hills. We erected the flysheet of the tent and sat down in the tiny bit of shade to wait. The locals drifted away to where they had come from. Presumably they wouldn't return until things got interesting again – or we were little piles of bleached bones.

Three hours later, a moving plume of dust signalled that our hero was returning. He pulled up, dropped his bike on its side... and produced from his pocket a little collection of perfectly-threaded bolts. What a man! The total charge for this astonishing roadside service was a little under two shillings (12p). We doubled it and gave him my pen, a battered paperback novel and Stephen's comb. He seemed pleased and we were delighted. Lots of hand-shaking and grins, then we re-fitted the clutch, kick-started the bike and set off again – this time into an exotic new world.

So far on this journey the appearance of people and towns had changed very gradually as we travelled from place to place. Venice was an obvious anachronism and a total surprise, but most red-roofed Italian towns could meld into red-roofed Dalmatian towns with little noticeable difference except for language. And Croatian, Kosovan, Greek or Turkish farms looked very, very similar. The differences between a town in the Austrian Tyrol and a Greek fishing village were obvious, but when the comparisons were limited to the distance a battered old bike could trundle in a day, the changes in the way people lived and looked became quite subtle.

Istanbul was instantly and profoundly different.

When we drove the bikes along the banks of the Golden Horn and looked around, it felt as if we'd leapt into the East of the Arabian Nights. In the Sixties, there were then almost no Mosques in Britain, and now all about us the skyline was pierced by dozens of minarets rising above magnificent domes. Amongst the throngs of people, a veiled woman walked alongside a man in a Fez; hawkers served water in tiny, chained brass cups from brightly decorated tanks on their backs; beautiful but incomprehensible calligraphy was carved into old walls; there were fishermen cooking and selling their catch on the waterfront; and stalls selling spices, sweetmeats and stuffed vine leaves. This was a culture-shock for a bunch of English lads, and we loved it.

For the next few days, we were woken in our narrow beds by the call to prayer from the tiny mosque opposite the dormitory of our student's hostel. We had a breakfast of peaches, bread and sweet mint tea, then tramped around the city – from the Blue Mosque and the Hagia Sophia to the Grand Bazaar and Topkapi Palace. It was during those long walks through the maze of ancient streets that I realized Steve was weird. He knew, by a sort of topographic osmosis, where all these places were. I could turn two corners and get lost in moments, but he always seemed to know which way to go, like a homing pigeon. It was very handy, but when he looked at me with puzzled incomprehension at my geographical hopelessness, it was also infuriating.

Istanbul was suffering from an acute water shortage that summer, and each area of the city was allowed access to the mains for only two hours every day. That inevitably led to a crush for the bathrooms and lavatories, and while queueing each time, we became friendly with a group of young Germans. Despite not speaking much of each other's languages – 'Guten Morgan', plus the sort of phrases film and comic-book

Nazi storm-troopers shouted, aren't sufficient to build a deep acquaintanceship – we got on perfectly well. Until the thirtieth of July in the late afternoon, when they just stopped speaking to us. We were ignored, cut, blanked, and rather puzzled. What had we done? It was only much later, in a letter from Dad collected at Damascus, that it became obvious what had gone wrong: our German friends found out that England had won the World Cup against their team and they were peeved.

Whatever the reason for their Germanic huff, it didn't matter much because it felt time to leave them and Istanbul behind – and that meant we needed to find a new set of tools.

The Grand Bazaar sold spices, jewellery, brocades, ancient flintlocks, even plastic ducks, but no tyre levers or spanners. And in the main streets of the town there were some stores that stocked very expensive, imported toolkits. But for equipment in our price range, we had to travel to a local market out beyond the city walls. There, amongst scores of shifty men who pulled at our clothes and hissed "You wanna change money?", were traders selling everything from onions to second-hand false teeth. We foraged around to make up a basic replacement kit. Our stolen tools had been battered and rusty, but forged out of good metal by proper craftsmen – sadly, when we eventually had our first repair to do and removed this new stuff from their card backings and shiny plastic bubbles, it became evident that they had been made by casting a toffee-like substance into moulds. Edges instantly wore away and surfaces bent and cracked under pressure...not an impressive investment in the bike's future.

But we were happily ignorant of this as we headed down to the Bosphorus ferry – and a new continent.

"This is where the journey really begins". Stephen had said this when we set off south from the Jowett's prefab in Nottingham, and then repeated it as we drove off the ferry in Calais. Mike said it when we left Europe and crossed into Communist Jugoslavia and the Balkans. After that it became a catchphrase, whether we were starting off on a new phase of our travels or even popping into the bushes for a pee. But this was a big stride – we were crossing to another continent, leaving Europe and entering Asia.

So, as the boat chugged away across the Bosphorus and headed for Scutari on the opposite bank, we all said it together.

SEVEN: *The Great Anatolian Plain*

At first the road to Ankara ran through rich, well-irrigated agricultural land. Our little convoy puttered past mile upon mile of small farms growing fruit, wheat and maize under a very hot August sun.

Travelling on a moving bike through most of Europe, even on the warmest day, had been pleasantly cool, but as we got further south it became increasingly like facing into a warm hairdryer. So, at the market place in a small town, we bought lengths of white fabric and some wide brown cotton tape. These were botched into a pastiche of Bedouin headdresses. They stopped us getting heatstroke and, we thought, looked pretty damn dashing.

The heat also made us constantly thirsty, and passing acres of succulent, ripe fruit was an ongoing temptation. For a long time we didn't weaken – just licked our lips and drove on by. Then eventually, at a seemingly deserted field overflowing with big, ripe watermelons, we succumbed to our thirst, stopped the bikes and car, and nonchalantly strolled across to the closest fruits. I was bending over a big one with my knife poised when, far away, I heard a shout and a bang. I looked up and there was a farmer in the distance yelling and waving a shotgun, and all my brave friends were legging it back to the vehicles. The Matchless and Ford started up and quickly pulled away. Mike reached the Ariel first and leapt on the kick-start. It didn't fire. He tried again. And again. With an armed and angry landowner marching towards us, this was a bad time for the bike to be difficult. Then it backfired loudly, twice, and the man halted and started to reload. I think he may have thought we were firing back and our scrumping expedition was turning into the Gunfight at the O.K.

Corral. At last, after another kick, the bike farted a cloud of black smoke and then began to run smoothly. We leapt onboard and pulled away as fast as we could go. After that we all went back to buying our fruit honestly.

Just to compound our guilt at the attempted melon robbery: the following evening we stopped the vehicles and lay down in our sleeping bags on a rough verge by the side of the road. Alongside us was a rose hedge, surrounding a nearby school. At sun-up the next day, we each became aware of a couple of male figures moving around and about us. Eventually one of the men coughed loudly to attract our attention. We leapt up, assuming that either the melon farmer had caught up with us, or that we had camped in an undesirable spot and were about to be moved on again. But instead, we were each presented with a rose, a handshake and a broad grin. One of the nicest awakenings I've ever had.

Over the next hundred miles the landscape became parched and even hotter as we began to cross the Great Anatolian Plain. Smallholdings growing many different crops gave way to huge wheat fields or wild, bleached-ochre grasslands. Trees became rare and the tallest vegetation was scrubby thorn bushes. It was the sort of landscape that would be a fine backdrop for the Mongol Hordes. Or, with our single black ribbon of road arrowing towards the horizon, an alternative location for The Great American Road Movie.

The wheat was ready for harvest and we often passed whole families gathering their crop. Every generation seemed to be there for the task, from Grannies and Granddads down to the tiniest infants. But there was rarely a farmhouse or any means of transport in sight, so how they all arrived there was anyone's guess. And there were no machines to help with the work – scythes and wooden rakes were used to cut and move the crop. Then the threshing was done by a man wearing goggles, standing on and driving a heavy wooden sled pulled by two horses. This crushed the wheat seeds from the stalk, and he was followed by women with wooden forks tossing up the chaff to be blown away in the faint breeze.

On the long straight road we could be seen coming for miles, and as we were 'the only show in town' – the only other human life they saw for hours at a time – we would be waved and cheered as we chugged past. Sometimes we were made to stop and shake hands with the entire workforce – sudden celebrities whose only claim to fame was that we happened to be passing and looked different from the usual traffic. Roger's height and Pat and Mike's red hair always fascinated the adults while the kids would clamber all over the sidecars and bikes, trying on our sunglasses and wiggling the handlebars.

This was usually fun, until one family insisted that we took a look at their daughter. We were ushered towards a young girl in a headscarf, who looked about nine or ten and quite terrified of the sudden attention. Her Dad shoved his big dirty thumb on her chin and the other hand on her forehead, forcing her head back and her mouth open. Mum pointed to show that we should look inside. A tooth was growing down through the centre of her palette and must have been very uncomfortable. They expected us to help her – to pull it out. The idea of one of us using a pair of our pliers on the little girl's dodgy molar, whilst presumably the rest of us held her down, was horrifying – the tooth might have been in the wrong place, but it was very solidly rooted. Without anaesthetic (and a Degree in Dentistry), it would have been excruciating to yank away at it, especially with pliers bought in the Istanbul market.

So we gave her one of our aspirins and, sensing the family's disappointment, left rather sheepishly, feeling thoroughly useless. What was the use being a mini-celebrity if you couldn't work miracles? After that we were more reticent about stopping in case we were asked to remove an appendix, deliver a baby or marry their cousin. It was always good to try new experiences, but there was a limit...somewhere short of surgery or weddings.

EIGHT: *Breakdown*

In the 1920s, when Kemal Ataturk overthrew the last of the Ottomans and founded the modern Turkish Republic, he decided that Istanbul would no longer be the Capital. It was tainted with the decadence of the old regime and too vulnerable to attack from the Dardanelles and Black Sea. Instead, he declared Ankara to be the new seat of government. It sits isolated on the great, wide Anatolian Plain, blown by bitter east winds in the winter and baked to a dry husk in the summer. The civil servants who survived the General's coup must have cursed their luck when they were forced to move from their civilized, cosmopolitan life on the Bosphorus to this desolate place. It had all the trappings of a Capital city – wide, straight roads, imposing buildings, fountains, and an air of importance, but no idiosyncrasies or atmosphere. It seemed a manufactured entity rather than a place that had developed and grown over generations.

We came into Ankara from the west on our ailing Ariel, and, while searching for the route south, found ourselves driving up towards the Presidential Palace. The central divide up the long Avenue Ataturk had soldiers on sentry-duty posted every fifty yards or so. We were dusty and grubby, but dressed in our ex-army desert jackets and pseudo-Bedouin headdresses, on a motorbike combination with a vaguely military air about it and a Union Jack on the hatch cover. The first sentry glanced at us, hesitated, then snapped to heel-stamping attention. The second soldier decided to play it safe and go along with his mate. That set the pattern and we were saluted all the way up to the Palace. We solemnly raised our hands to our foreheads each time, and the bike acknowledged the compliment by backfiring loudly and blowing out clouds of black smoke. I think we did Her Majesty proud.

Feeling absurdly chuffed by the farce we'd just appeared in, we drove through the outskirts and were soon crossing the wild, flat grasslands again, heading south towards the distant Syrian frontier. All day, despite the good straight road and flat terrain, the bike travelled very slowly, coughing, spluttering and misfiring constantly. We crawled along the shores of Lake Tuz Golu, and after another twenty miles finally ground to a halt on a desolate stretch of road.

Inside the engine housing, the two timing gears that regulated the opening and shutting of the valves were stripped of their teeth and the chain that connected and regulated them was in a little heap at the bottom of the casing. By then the sun was setting, and, suspecting that we would be there for quite some time, we dispiritedly climbed into our sleeping bags.

The next two weeks were the low point of the journey, marred by squalor, tedium and disappointment.

It started well when the Matchless and the Ford found us. Pat and Roger decided that, however long it took, they would stop and help. This was a generous decision and one which we three will always have reasons to be very grateful for, because it involved them making several trips backwards and forwards to Ankara and the loss of a great deal of good travelling time. For us, having these people to support us gave us heart and meant we stood some chance of being able to carry on with the journey in one way or another. Without them we would have been in an impossible position, stuck on a desolate stretch of road without any means of summoning help or organising what happened next.

Another small beacon of hope was that we had our

spare-parts insurance policy, and that meant new timing gears could be sent for from the Automobile Association.

Mike climbed on the Matchless behind his brother and set off back to the City to send a telegram to London, and at the end of that day they returned with the news that the AA had acknowledged our message and would find and dispatch the spares to us by airfreight as quickly as possible. They estimated it would take about five or six days.

The Ariel couldn't go anywhere under its own power, and as it contained all our stuff, we could only stay with it by the side of that long, empty stretch of road. The three tents were put up to provide a bit of shade, and we began an interminable argument about what to do. Steve showed his ability to accept a hard truth and was all for cutting our losses, giving up on the bike immediately and starting to hitch. Mike and I disagreed. We wanted to stay together on TOF 80 as long as possible, hopefully all the way to Jerusalem. So with our disagreements ebbing to-and-fro, we settled down to wait.

Six days on a featureless, hot plain with nothing to do is a very long time. As an only child I thought I knew how to deal with boredom, but this was taking it to a whole new level of pointlessness. Eventually we all began to adapt, shut down our expectations of novelty and went into a sort of zen-state, lying around, half-asleep, watching an occasional bird wheeling about high above, or a lorry passing. Sometimes the 'what-to-do-next' argument would rumble about, or a desultory conversation would start up:

Which woman we'd save, if humanity was almost wiped out, to help us in the task of re-populating the earth. (This was the height of the Cold War and the Cuban Missile Crisis had threatened to put an end to the world four years previously, so featuring in an Adam and Eve scenario seemed a real possibility).

Or how we longed for beans on toast, and which Birmingham or Nottingham fish and chip shop was the best.

Deep philosophical stuff.

When we ran short of real food someone would drive the Matchless off to the nearest village, some twenty miles away, and buy a few basic commodities to keep us going. Once a small boy appeared from over the horizon, carrying a large flatbread which he offered to sell us. We were delighted with the bread and particularly with the idea that someone had found us in that wilderness. We probably paid far too much, because within a couple of hours he was back, this time with a live chicken, which he offered to slaughter there and then. We squeamishly refused the bargain and didn't see the disappointed salesman again.

There was no water in that desolate spot, it had to be brought in bottles and was therefore reserved for drinking only. So neither our bodies nor our clothes were clean. Even washing our hands after 'going off into the wilderness' didn't happen much, and that, presumably was why each of us, one after the other, went down with diarrhoea. There were no large leaves around to wipe our bums with; no one fancied using the thorn bushes; and what little lavatory paper we owned was very quickly gone. That's where the AA route guides went, and then the pages of our diaries. As our bowels became more and more troubled, so our mood darkened and our optimism diminished. By the time the six days were up we were convinced the journey for us three was over. It was time to give up and head home. This was compounded when a visit to the Post Office produced no parcel from England. They suggested we try again in a couple of days.

On the next trip into Ankara the spares were there, and when Steve and Pat returned with them, our moods instantly brightened and we all danced around as much as our sphincters would allow. The replacement timing gears, which cost fourteen shillings, had a further five pounds in customs duty slapped on them and were lighter and quite insubstantial compared to the originals. But they fitted, and when we kick-started the bike it leapt into life, running smoothly.

Our campsite had become a slum over those eight days, but very quickly everything was packed and tidied away. And with a song in our hearts and a rumble in our bowels, we rode away from that dismal place, surrounded by its myriad lavatorial mounds of turned earth.

Ten minutes down the road, the bike backfired again and then stopped with a clunk. The new, long-awaited gears had stripped their teeth and we were back in the same mire. Everyone became silent, Steve squatted down, head in hands, and I walked off a little way. We were too disappointed and demoralized for swearing or histrionics.

Mike just sat on the bike seat, pondering for some minutes, then looked around and said the unthinkable: the damage to the replacements probably meant that they were a symptom rather than the real problem. Some deeper fault was causing them to fail, therefore there was no point in contacting the AA again for a repeat prescription. It would cost us more than we could afford in import tax, and, more importantly, would mean an interminable wait at a new but equally awful roadside camp, probably for the same thing to happen in another five miles. After a few lame counter arguments from me and a minute or two of coming to terms with this frightening logic, I had to agree. It meant that TOF 80 was finished and, if we'd listened to

Steve, we'd have been a great deal nearer the Holy Land by then.

For me, and I think for Mike, the demise of the bike was like losing a talisman and a precious security blanket – it had given us independence, freedom and confidence. We had basked in the attention it received as it chugged, rattled and backfired across two-and-a-half thousand miles, and we had seen remarkable and exciting things from those three seats.

But keeping it going had become an end in itself – an obsessive habit increasingly hard to sustain. Recently, as the bike became more and more troubled, the real reason for travelling had been almost forgotten and life had been about nursing the engine along for a few more miles. The machine had become the journey.

NINE: *Goodbye to TOF 80*

As we sat around trying to make the best of things, it began to dawn, even on me, that though our transport had gone, the journey needn't be over. We convinced ourselves that we now had a new sort of freedom. We would stick out our thumbs and become three simple hitch-hikers. Hopefully we could still make it to Jerusalem, or even further.

But all this group positivism and enthusiasm tended to evaporate away in the quiet, lonely hours before dawn. I would lie awake in my sleeping bag, fearful that our lives were about to turn into a nightmare of interminable waits on lonely roads, or violent confrontations with malevolent motorists. During our late-teens Steve and I had done enough hitching in Europe to know that, whilst most people were very pleasant and glad to help a couple of young lads on their way, it was possible to come across an oddity who was unpleasant. It only needed one nutter to make life suddenly very difficult. Silently fretting about imagined horrors yet to come was a bad way to spend the night, so it was always a relief when the sun nudged up over the distant hills. Then we were too busy sorting out the bike and all of our luggage for me to worry about the future.

At first we thought that the Ariel could be handed over to the nearest blacksmith to be made use of. Just walking away from all our mechanical problems, leaving the locals to find some use for the old Brummagem wreck, seemed an attractive notion. If they couldn't get it going, then they'd find a myriad of inventive uses for all the bits. However, this sensible, eco-friendly solution wouldn't have met with the approval of the Turkish Customs at the border. When we entered the country we had been registered as travelling with a vehicle. If we now tried to leave on foot, they would assume that we had sold it without paying Import Duty. Avoiding this sort of problem meant yet more journeys back to Ankara and, with the help of the British Consul, having TOF 80 taken off our papers, then arranging for it be towed away for 'official' disposal. This cost far more money than we could afford, but there was no choice. The Turkish Authorities were not people to get on the wrong side of. We'd heard in the Istanbul hostel what they did to drug-runners, and presumably bike-smugglers.

Pat and Roger continued to be the best possible comrades during the bike's final days, but they must have been relieved to see the back of our old wreck. Helping us had cost them so many long days of boredom, sitting by the side of that desolate road, or running us to and from Ankara to sort the problems out. Now at least they got the chance to pick over the bones of our outfit. They stripped the Ariel down to provide their bike with some useful spares. But, best of all, the big lumpy Watsonian sidecar was taken off their Matchless and replaced with our stylish little fiberglass number. I changed the lettering to read 'Nottingham to Jerusalem', and this gave us a tiny bit of satisfaction, because it was a way of saying Thanks - and also meant that a portion of our outfit might make it all the way to the Holy Land.

'Succeed or Bust' as the Cyrillic lettering on the side pretended to say.

Five days after TOF 80 clunked to its final halt, we watched as it was loaded onto a truck and driven away to the breaker's yard. No one said anything. I think a single word would have reduced me to tears. Then, after we had shaken hands with Pat and Roger, they started their bike and drove away, along that very straight road towards distant Syria.

We were left, a trio of tiny figures on the huge Anatolian Plain, to pick up our backpacks and start walking after them.

Two hours later, we were bouncing around in the back of a noisy lorry, heading south and feeling much happier.

TEN: *The Lebanon*

If he is going to get anywhere, a hitch-hiker quickly learns a few useful guidelines:

Three young blokes seem too threatening to be picked up by a lone driver. A double act stands more chance, but single hitchers are consistently more successful.

A tractor might be slow, but any progress in the right direction is better than standing at the roadside.

Borders are almost impossible to hitch through. No one wants take a stranger into another country, particularly if there's political tension. It's best to get a bus or taxi from the nearest town to the customs post, walk through the checkpoint, change money into the local currency, and then start looking for a new lift.

Being a pillion passenger on a motorbike whilst wearing a heavy backpack is a cruel and unusual punishment; when you bounce up, your luggage goes down – and vice-versa. After a few miles your shoulders are sawn through and your arms fall off.

Sadly I was never given a lift by a gorgeous woman who decided to make me her plaything, and I generally disbelieve other travellers who told me it happened to them. I think it comes under the heading 'wishful thinking'. There were however a couple of offers from Arab gentlemen (which were politely refused). Mike and I discovered that travelling in shorts wasn't a good idea. We only did it once and were besieged with interesting offers. Throughout a thirty-mile journey, one insistent fellow passenger on the bus offered us the opportunity to visit his garden, where, he assured us, many young Englishmen had enjoyably gone jig-a-jig-jig before.

There's rarely such thing as a free lift. A hitch-hiker

often pays his fare by being a good listener and this can usually be interesting, and a great way to find out about the place you're travelling through. But occasionally it can be hard work. For example, a man in an expensive motorcar who offers a lift is often out to show off his grasp of your language, his opinions and his status – even to scruffy travellers like us. And sometimes, if one is of a vaguely liberal, pinkish turn of mind, these successful men hold views that are hard to listen to, but if you are philosophical and content to sit quietly, whilst disagreeing inwardly, they are the price for the swift and comfortable miles covered. By acting as a sounding-board and a nodding dog, you are getting nearer your destination. However, just occasionally it can become too big a price. Then, following a short and hopefully polite disagreement, you get out and wait for another lift.

Most people, however, were friendly and surprisingly helpful to young lads they didn't know and had no real reason to care about. Sometimes, after sticking out the thumb, lifts came in minutes; at other times we would wait for hours. Eventually, if all else failed, for a tiny amount of money there were other modes of transport. In a country where there aren't reliable long-distance buses, shared taxis and minibuses offer a very cheap alternative. Cheaper still, lorries will often provide a useful unscheduled service. On the return journey from delivering his load, the driver will fill up, inside and out, with anyone who has a few coins.

In southern Turkey, all through the hours of darkness, we travelled across the Taurus Mountains in a large open lorry. The three of us had paid our money and then jumped up into a completely empty back. But soon the lorry stopped again and a man and his wife threw a huge amount of baggage in with us and, before climbing on board, heaved and pushed up the two donkeys that had been carrying it all. Over the next dozen miles we were joined by a veiled old lady, a goat, several trussed chickens, two small children, dozens of wicker baskets, several sacks of grain and three heavily-bearded men, one with a large knife in his waistband. He grinned when he invited me to test the sharpness of the blade, and what little light there was glinted on his gold teeth. Not a restful night, but as the dawn came up we crossed through the Cilician Gates, then roared downhill with the brakes squealing towards the city of Adana and that elusive Syrian frontier.

After crossing the immensity of Turkey, travelling around the countries of the Mediterranean Middle East quickly brings home the fact that, despite their political, tactical and historical importance – and the noise they make on the World-stage – they are all very small. Even hitchhiking, it doesn't take long to nip between Syria, Lebanon, Jordan, and even Israel. Only the politics make it slower, more complicated, or impossible.

Over the next few days, together and separately, we hitched in and out of towns with names straight out of St Paul's Epistles or the Tales of the Crusaders: Alexandretta; Antioch; Tartus; Latakia. But they all seemed dismal places, not worth breaking our progress for – just dust and concrete. We slept when it was too dark to hitch or when we were too tired to travel any further that day. One night after travelling alone, I shared the floor of a dirty hut with a young bloke from Canterbury. He was on his way back from Pakistan and Afghanistan, where I suspect he'd been sampling the poppy products. I was very scruffy by then, but, by his lack of everything, he made me feel over-privileged. He was gaunt, spoke very slowly, hesitating over each word, and all he owned were the vest, shorts and sandals he was wearing, plus a battered military bugle that he wouldn't put down for a moment. There may have been some illegal souvenirs of the Orient stuffed up its tubes, but it seemed intrusive to ask. Despite being robbed several times and beaten up once, he had managed to hitch across both Iran and Iraq and was then heading up through Turkey to Europe and home – quite a traveller. We shared the little bit of food that I had, and when I woke the next morning he'd gone, along with one of my dirty shirts.

At last we crossed briefly into the top corner of Syria – then within a day's travel were out again and into Lebanon. This was many years before it was torn apart by the savage civil war of 1975, and it was then a modern, cosmopolitan country with an air of colonial sophistication. Lebanon had become independent from France twenty years before, but retained an air of savoir-faire and was the Middle Eastern playground of the stylish Med-set. But fortunately, despite this, there were a few cheap hostels for poor travellers. The three of us met up then rented cut-price dormitory beds in Tripoli. We thankfully washed ourselves and our clothes and rejoiced in the luxury of a lavatory that, while not very clean, disposed of its contents without any digging.

Then, feeling a bit more civilized and certainly smelling sweeter, we went off to do a bit of 'style-watching' – walking along a harbour graced by exquisite yachts and beautiful people.

Everyone spoke either French or Arabic, so when, at a coffee house next morning, a pleasant, middle-aged Priest started a conversation, the limitations of even Mike's school language lessons were quickly passed. Father Sebastian was plump, dressed in a grubby cassock and had no English. But he did have a car and told us – in the combination of mime and Euro-speak that is everyone's common tongue – that within the hour he was off into the mountains to visit a monastery. So in exchange for our assurance that we were good Catholic lads and loved Jesus, he would give us a lift up to the famous Cedars of Lebanon. It seemed an affordable price for a journey. "J'tadore Jesus" we all muttered in appalling accents and climbed aboard his tiny Fiat.

He dropped us at the small village of Bsharre near one of the largest and oldest group of Cedars – huge, elegant trees with limbs reaching out like canopies. For millennia they had been all over these slopes, but the Phoenicians, Romans and everyone else had enjoyed their straight and scented timber. So now there were just a few outcrops of precious survivors. That night we lay in our sleeping bags beneath the ancient branches.

In the misty dawn I woke suddenly aware of hot breath on my face and a rumbling noise. Fortunately I didn't shout or throw my arms about, just half-opened my sleepy, myopic eyes. Above me, poised over my face, were the teeth, jowls and yellow eyes of a huge hound. From where I was lying, looking up, it seemed as big as a bull and was wearing a wide, spiked iron collar. It didn't seem to like what it was sniffing, because a low growl rumbled around its throat. I froze, too petrified to do anything other than squint and tremble while it sniffed down the length of me and came back to my head. After a while it grew bored and quickly looked up, slobbering a string of drool across my mouth and chin, then, perhaps hoping for more entertainment, padded across to investigate my friends. As quietly as I could, I reached into the pocket of the rucksack alongside me and fumbled for my specs and lock knife. If it was going to tear our throats out, I was going to get in one desperate stab. Underneath the folds of my sleeping bag I clicked the blade open, and the dog heard the noise. It started back towards me, growling louder this time. I sat up, knife in hand – a weedy Brummy designer versus the Hound of the Baskervilles – 'Oh shit'.

From way away, invisible in the mist, a man called out. The dog stopped, listened, looked back at me, torn between a tasty snack and obedience, then turned and lolloped off towards the voice.

This was no way to start the morning, especially for someone with dodgy bowels.

ELEVEN: *Damascus*

The next couple of days were dogless and delightful. In the clean, crisp air of Mount Lebanon, we scrambled over the peaks and slopes, enjoying great views across the Bequaa Valley.

In the winter, these were the ski-runs for the smart-set. It was said that one could water-ski in the Med, have an early lunch in a fine Beirut restaurant, then, with the services of a fast car, be snow-skiing up here by mid-afternoon.

But we were there in high, hot summer and the place was deserted. One of my faded 35mm slides shows Mike and Steve on top of the world in brilliant sunshine, making a tomato sandwich from large flatbread. They look thin but content.

Time to move on again. Down from the peace of the mountains into the mad bustle of Lebanon's Capital. Beirut was then the centre of trade for the whole Eastern Mediterranean – anything or anyone could be bought and sold there – and, alongside the beautiful people, the streets heaved with merchants, crooks, pimps, money-changers and all the parasites and bottom-feeders that lived alongside and off them. Fortunately we didn't provide much in the way of temptation at any level for the local sharks, and so passed our time there unnoticed and unscathed until it was time to hit the road east to Damascus.

Historians reckon that the Syrian capital was first settled about four thousand years ago, which makes it amongst the world's oldest continuously-inhabited cities. When we arrived it was looking its age – fascinating but a bit down-at-heel and tatty. So we fitted in pretty well.

In a cheap rooming house in the Old Town, we sat

on unwholesome beds and reviewed our situation: due to lack of hygiene and an odd diet, all three of us had dodgy bowels and, as a result, had lost all the comfortable city-fat we'd set out with and were getting decidedly thin. But despite that and our hit-and-miss methods of travel, an itinerant existence had now become normal and we liked it. Just carrying on travelling was a very simple and satisfying way of life – no real responsibilities, except thumbing a lift and heading to the next town.

A more urgent problem was a shortage of money, partly because of the fees incurred at Turkish Customs when getting rid of TOF 80, but mainly because we hadn't started out from England with very much. I suspect that optimism, as usual, had led us to believe that what cash we had would go a great deal further than it did.

I was a bit better off than the other two, having been a wage earner, rather than a student, and my dependable and lovely Mom and Dad had slipped me a folded tenner just before we left. This was now hidden deep in my rucksack underneath some unpleasant underwear. Despite this lavish contingency fund, we all knew that the time had come to realise whatever qualities or skills we had and try to raise some cash. We discussed trekking round the local Restaurants asking for work as washers-up or, if any Patron was daft enough to contemplate it, as waiters.

Fortunately a fellow traveller, lying on another seedy bed further down the large room we were in, overheard our conversation and had a suggestion that was intriguing because it didn't involve any real work. Hospitals in Syria, he said, were happy to pay good money for blood 'donations'. Someone he knew had met someone on a bus, whose friend had been paid a small fortune for a particularly rare blood group.

Sounded good to us. But he also warned us to be wary of having dirty, second-hand needles shoved in our arms, so we chose to donate at The American Hospital, because it sounded 'Western' and might therefore be hygienic.

Walking through the souks on our way there, we decided that whatever the outcome – if hopefully one of us had a particularly expensive blend of gore – the money would be shared out equally.

The hospital was hard to find, tucked away in a maze of alleyways and bearing no resemblance to the sort of streamlined establishment we'd seen in American movies. No gates and long driveway up to a gleaming glass atrium, the entrance was between a clothes stall and a butcher's shop, and the disembodied gaze of a skinned sheep's head followed us up the steps and into a grimy hallway.

A receptionist took one look at us and pointed down a corridor – she had seen plenty of our sort before and knew exactly why we were there. After negotiating our way past a man disconsolately dragging a mop across a dried bloodstain on the floor tiles, we found ourselves in a waiting room. There was no window, just a fizzing fluorescent tube and a ceiling fan slowly revolving overhead. Around the walls were a few poor Arabs and some European blokes who looked a lot like us – thin and slightly needy, perched on a random collection of ramshackle chairs. One by one they were called up to a plywood desk to have their blood assessed.

Soon it was our turn and we were each stabbed on a finger. The resulting red blob dropped into some clear liquid. Other tests were done on the three samples, then Mike and I were told that we had very ordinary blood, but the doctors could be persuaded to purchase some of it for a small sum. Steve's blood, on the other hand, was a different matter. Our ears pricked up. Were we all in the money? Was he as unique as he was always telling us?

No. It seemed that his hemoglobin level was too low to be of any use. His veins carried something resembling warm water with no commercial viability whatsoever. So, as we were taken through a curtain to the draining room, he went back to his seat with something resembling a grin at the corners of his bloodless lips.

The Syrian system of blood-letting was different to what we were used to in the NHS. We were each told to lie on stained leather couches and to push our arms through a hole in the wall up to the shoulder. A black drape was then pulled across the hole so it wasn't possible to see what was going on beyond. Hands grabbed our arms and a stern, disembodied woman's voice told us to 'clinch fist!'. There was a bit of pummelling and a slap followed by a sharp stab near the inside of the elbow. We then lay there for a long time as, presumably, an unspecified number of jugs and basins were filled with our blood.

Eventually we were given our arms back and, feeling quite dizzy, told to get up and go to another hole, where wodges of dirty Syrian banknotes were pushed through at us. No cup of tea or biscuit, just the blood-money and the transaction was complete.

Stephen was outside waiting for us, still trying to keep a straight face. And what was left of our blood boiled when he suggested we find a coffee house so we could divide up the money three ways, as per the agreement. We told him what we thought of him, his hemoglobin and our recent deal. And after we had finished our rant, his expression changed to hurt and puzzlement, then there was a short pause, and all three of us grinned and went to find the coffee. It didn't occur to any of us that his symptoms might show that he was very run down and possibly on the edge of proper illness. It just seemed the perfect excuse for him to avoid Vlad the Impaler.

The next day, with our small bundles of Syrian Pounds burning holes in our pockets, we decided to buy souvenirs for the folks back home. The first part of the day was spent strolling around Saladin's Tomb, meandering through Al-Hamidiyah Souq and along the Street called Straight – looking at the tourist tat on offer – and tittering at small models of Saint Paul in a Basket (complete with a length of rope to lower him to safety) made to commemorate his escape from the Damascus Zealots in the first century.

Then the day's second part was spent with me in a state of barely-controlled hysteria, while we searched most of Damascus for my lost passport. (We had to carry passports with us, because Syria was a Police State and anyone might be stopped and asked for ID – and before any tourist could make a purchase in a shop, they had to produce documentary proof of their existence).

The drama started after hours of wandering around the maze of markets, alleyways and souks, when I realised my precious little blue book wasn't in my pocket anymore. I instantly went into a cold sweat and ran frantically between the last few stalls and shops we'd browsed. What had started as a pleasant day of shopping had, for me, turned into a nightmare. A British Passport was then a saleable item on the black market, and without it, my only course of action was to present myself at the UK Embassy, and, having hopefully proved who I was, be given some sort of basic documentation, which would only get me back to England, a minefield of snotty bureaucracy, followed by an ignominious return to 'go'.

After watching me do the headless-chicken-act for

a while, my two friends stopped me and said we must be systematic and re-trace our steps logically. I was never strong on logic, and now I had run around a few alleys I wasn't even sure which way was up.

Fortunately, however, we had Steve's inbuilt sat nav. He went into a slight trance and then set off, almost sniffing the ground. We followed, with Mike nodding and muttering that he remembered this place and that shop, but I could have been in Calcutta for all I recognized. A normal state of personal disorientation combined with mild panic isn't a good aid to topographic awareness.

After what seemed an awful long time, Steve turned into yet another narrow street, froze, and then, like some sort of conjuror, raised his arm to point at a shop window. There, upright in front of a display of old brass lamps and antique swords, was my precious passport.

Almost instantly, the mists in my brain cleared and I remembered exactly what had happened hours earlier. The shopkeeper was a Jew called Moses and, when we'd dropped in for a nose around, he'd been very patient and welcoming. He knew we weren't going to buy the bronze casket we all studied carefully – we had neither the money nor the means to transport it away – but he went through the motions of showing us its finer points, and when we said we liked it, applauded our good taste. Eventually we bought a few postcards, and I think at that point I had taken my passport out and put it down on the counter, while I searched for coins in the same pocket. Soon after we left, he had found it and put it in the window, hoping we'd pass that way again.

He seemed a good, kind man, and he saved me from an ignominious end to my travels. I hope he came safely through the terrors of the following year, 1967, when Syria, along with its Arab neighbours, tried and failed to smash the Jewish State. Living right in the heart of Israel's most vehement enemy was a difficult and dangerous place for anybody called Moses.

I went through the third part of the day in a state of mild euphoria, delighted with my good luck, at the kindness of strangers, and, yet again, astonished at the magic compass lodged in Steve's brain.

And then, just to round off the afternoon, we even managed some serious shopping at a carpenter's yard. He sold furniture encrusted with tiny pieces of bone, mother of pearl, cedar, sandal and olive wood. Showy but rather stylish, we all thought.

I bought two inlaid boxes for Janet and Mom, and, for cousin Dave, a fearsome Bedouin whip of plaited leather, whose handle unscrewed to reveal a vicious metal spike. (When, back in Brum, I gave it to him, his Mother was horrified, convinced I had set him on a road to violence and eventual incarceration. She made sure it disappeared quite quickly).

Mom's Damascus box is still around, and after forty-odd years, has its inlay intact. It now rests on the mantelpiece of our back bedroom and contains her rosary beads, wristwatch and wedding ring, returned to us by the funeral directors after her cremation.

Stephen put almost all his blood-money – or his share of *our* blood-money – as a healthy deposit on a large and expensive inlaid games-table for his Mother. Sensible as always, Mike asked him how he intended to carry it home. At this point the carpenter jumped in, assuring Steve that, as soon as the balance was paid, the table would be shipped, at the shop's expense, to anywhere Mrs. Byrne desired. I took a couple of photos to show her what a prize she was about to receive, then we wended our way, like three men who'd just purchased a Byrne Family heirloom.

I gather, when Steve's Mum was later shown the

pictures, she said it was possibly the most vulgar piece of furniture she'd ever seen.

TWELVE: *Jordan*

Two days later we were over another border, into Jordan, and at last we'd reached the 'Holy Land' proper.

Mike and I were hitching together, and a few miles beyond the Customs Post we were offered a lift by a well-fed, sleek young man of about twenty, driving a smart motor. He was the son of a lawyer and was keen to practice his English. He told us that his family was originally from Jaffa – now in Israel. Then he asked why we British had abandoned the Arab people in 1948 and allowed the Zionists to steal their homes. Before long, our wafer-thin understanding of the Palestinian Mandate was drained, leaving him with no useful answers and us with the feeling that our grasp of Middle-East affairs, skimmed from the English media, was both lightweight and one-sided. He soon realised that he was dealing with political naivety on an impressive scale, accepted our personal apologies for mishandling the withdrawal of our forces eighteen years before (when we were four), and politely changed the conversation to something he thought we could handle.

Despite his splendid car and general air of well-being, he felt his Father was not generous with his allowance, so he asked how we had persuaded our parents to pay for all our travelling. We told him they were quite poor and that we were funding ourselves from earnings and savings. The novelty of this either intrigued him, or he took pity on us, so when we reached the spot where he should have dropped us off, he asked instead if we'd like to go to his home for lunch. We were long past being coy about offers of food and accepted cheerfully.

The house was large, with patterned Islamic tiles up to window height, then ochre stucco and a castellated roofline. It was surrounded by decorative railings, enclosing a pretty, well-tended garden full of date-palms and flowering shrubs.

Once inside, our rucksacks were taken by an old servant and we were ushered into a shadowy, cool saloon and onto cushions arranged around a low table. After we had settled ourselves cross-legged, a bead curtain at the back of the room swished aside and two extremely attractive young women came in, carrying glasses of Coke on a polished brass tray, giggling and smiling shyly. One was about sixteen and dressed in Western clothes and the other a little older, but in traditional costume, with baggy, silk trousers, large earrings, lots of bracelets and bands of tiny, gold coins across her forehead. They were followed by an older lady who hushed them with a brusque word or two. Our host spoke quietly and firmly to the women, presumably telling them what was required, then they swished back through the curtain. He explained that they were his Mother and Sisters, and, while his Father was away in Amman, he was in charge.

After a while, the girls came back with a much larger tray, loaded with lamb, rice, salads, minty yoghurt and a platter of ripe, cool fruit. They placed it on the table and then disappeared back through the curtain. The man of the house explained that his older sister was dressed formally because she had recently become betrothed to the son of an important business contact of their Father. And until the wedding, she was expected to live in purdah – never going out, unless accompanied by her parents, and never, ever communicating with any young men. If she was seen in the company of a man she wasn't related to, her reputation would be ruined and neither she, nor her younger sister, would ever be considered marriageable again. The family would be tainted.

There was a short pause. Mike and I glanced at each other. Our host said that of course we didn't count, because we were a foreign novelty and would disappear in a few hours. Then he asked whether we minded if the girls came back through the curtain, practiced their English and asked us about our lives in the West. We weren't keen on his assessment of our irrelevance, but the idea of spending a couple of hours in the company of two charming young women seemed far nicer than tramping down a hot road, on a baking afternoon, hoping for a lift, so we happily agreed.

They were interested in The Beatles. They thought the boys looked quite beautiful, except the ugly drummer, but they dismissed their music as crude and noisy –Arabic love songs were far more soulful and beguiling.

Another fascination was how British girls met the boys they would eventually marry. They had read in newspapers that there was no system or rules, no involvement of the family elders – it just happened by chance. What a ridiculous way to run a romance.

They were two very incisive and witty women, and for two young men starved of female company it was a lovely afternoon. Even Mother softened a bit, and when we left she gave us a big smile and a bag of fruit – though I think she was relieved to see the back of us, with her family's reputation unsullied.

Our host dropped us a few miles from the Israeli frontier and the Sea of Galilee, on the outskirts of a little town called Irbid. As we strolled through the centre to get to the Amman road, I paused to watch a man in a Bedouin headdress smoking a hubble-bubble pipe outside a coffee house, and he spotted my fascination.

Since first seeing these large glass and brass devices in Istanbul, as a non-smoker, they had intrigued me. This time I was called across and offered the mouthpiece to try. I had no idea of the technique involved, so blew down the tube, watching the bubbles burst in the water, and then sucked hard. My lungs filled with vicious smoke, I went puce and nearly expired, coughing like an eighty-a-day man. Everyone at the surrounding tables fell about and slapped their knees at the sight of this weedy European doubled up from one puff. However, for the entertainment provided, and to help me recover, they gave us both a glass of water and a mint tea.

We did well for free food and drink that day.

THIRTEEN: *Jerusalem*

Many, many weeks before, by the side of a road in Austria, I had lettered down the length of our sidecar: 'Birmingham to Jerusalem – succeed or bust'. Now the three of us had met up again in Amman and were together on the last leg to the Old City, much thinner, minus the motorbike, but otherwise mostly unscathed.

The crowded, fume-filled Arab bus that brought us from the Jordanian Capital descended down through the Judean Hills, crossed the Allenby Bridge over the River Jordan, and, at dusk, finally stopped near the Damascus Gate. We pushed through the mass of other passengers to the exit, then the throng of people fighting to climb aboard, and stood for a moment, looking up at the walls of the town we'd come all this way to see – a place that was pivotal to Western history, revered by the three great monotheistic religions, and had been fought over, sacked and rebuilt since before the beginning of recorded history.

"Bloody good that – but I'm hungry," said Steve with just a hint of apathy.

"And thirsty," said Mike.

"And tired," I concluded.

So we picked up our rucksacks and strolled through the great archway to find somewhere to eat, drink and sleep.

The alleyways were just about wide enough for two loaded donkeys to pass, and the stones underfoot were smoothed by generations of feet. Everywhere there were signs for pilgrim hotels and hostels, but most looked too expensive. The dormitory we finally found turned out to be the most decrepit and filthy of the whole journey so far, but the city was full of tourists and the hostel-keeper made sure we'd paid five shillings each (25p) for two nights before we'd really seen the place. We were tired, so we reckoned we could put up with it – travellers with our levels of spending couldn't afford to be too fussy anyway. So we handed in our passports, accepted the elderly bed sheets shoved at us through the serving-hatch-cum-reception-desk and tramped up the winding stone stairway to the top floor.

There were about ten beds in the garret, most of them already occupied by huddled figures. The smell of unwashed bodies was strong and I daresay we quickly added to it. After covering the stained and grubby mattresses with the sheets, we took off our sandals and lay down.

Looking up at the vaulted, stone ceiling, we saw clusters of tiny insects moving around, then noticed that every so often they would seem to sense the rising heat of a human body beneath them, release their grip, and fall onto the sleeper below for a nibble. It was easy to deal with them while we were awake, but sooner or later our eyes closed, and the next morning we all had a considerable collection of large, itchy bites. Down the corridor, and shared by a horde of other travellers, was the lavatory: a single traditional-tiled hole in the floor with two raised footpads. It was a style we were well used to by then, but this hadn't been shown a mop (or a shovel), since Saladin ruled the City.

We moved to a slightly better hostel after our two-day tenancy expired.

In 1966 Jerusalem was a romantic and evocative place. With the exception of a small Israeli segment, it was a medieval Arab city – not in the sense that Bruges is medieval: neat, crisp, beautifully and painstakingly preserved – but in the sense that the drains were indistinguishable from how they would have smelt and functioned in the fourteenth century.

This wasn't the bronze-age capital of King David.

Or the city that Jesus and his followers knew – the Romans had reduced that to rubble in AD70.

It wasn't the place where the Byzantine Empress Helena had searched for the site of Christ's Calvary and the remnants of the true cross.

Or the prize the Crusaders took from the Saracens – or even the Ottoman Citadel.

And yet it seemed likely that if any one of its previous inhabitants had dropped by, they would have recognized at least bits of the old place. The past, as well as the plumbing, seeped through the stones.

The whole town, seen from up on the Mount of Olives, was a spectacular piece of set-design – a living embodiment of every Hollywood Biblical Epic we'd enjoyed or endured throughout our young lives. Looking down, it seemed possible that Charlton Heston could, at any moment, stroll around the corner on his way to share a flagon of wine with Vespasian, and all the extras from *The Greatest Story Ever Told* would have fitted into the crowds almost unnoticed. The flat-roofed limestone houses and shops were built all over each other and filled, higgledy-piggledy, every corner inside the walls, then spilled out over the surrounding low hills.

I recently saw a photo of those hills today, and they are covered with ugly multistory apartments, hotels and the tower-blocks of the Hebrew University. I'm sure the sanitation is better, but they do ruin the spectacle. That once-wonderful backdrop has turned into downtown Birmingham.

Before the defeat of the Arabs in the '67 war, and the subsequent erection of those suburban blots on the landscape, the biggest thing in town was the huge gold cupola of the Dome of the Rock – the third holiest mosque in the Muslim world. It got its name from the slab of stone in the centre of its massive, empty interior. This was the rock on which Abraham was about to sacrifice his son, until God told him it was only a joke, and it was from where Mohammed had ridden up to Paradise on his winged horse. The whole building is supposedly poised on top of the Earth's foundation stone and the cave where the Prophet of Islam went to meditate. Far below this is the 'Well of Souls', where the whispering of the dead can be heard mingling with the distant sound of the Rivers of Heaven falling into eternity...quite a notable spot.

Contentiously, the Mosque was built slap-bang in the middle of a great slabbed space where, two thousand years before, the Jewish Temple of Solomon had stood, with its Holy of Holies containing the Arc of the Covenant probably standing on Abraham's Rock. The western side of this giant courtyard is supported by the Wailing Wall, where Jews, banned by Jerusalem's Moslem rulers from praying at the site of their vanished temple, came to bemoan the loss of their homeland and the scattering of their tribes.

Finally, added to the inflammable mix were the many sects of Christians: Syrians; Coptics; Greeks; Ethiopians; Armenians; Russians; Roman Catholics and Anglicans, all constantly disputing with each other and everyone else over their rights to the Holy Places.

It was a setting primed to promote the bitterest sort of conflict. So we rarely saw any citizen walking around with a contented smile, happy to be in such a significant place. Jerusalem was full of barely-suppressed annoyance and knotted brows. People seemed peeved that everyone else didn't realise that this place was very special – to them! The owners of the multitude of gift shops seemed the most content – they had an unending flood of pilgrims bursting to buy their olivewood crucifixes and plastic Holy Sepulchres.

Someone once suggested that the Holy City, with all

its distilled anger and paranoia, was God's best argument for atheism. It was, and still is, a religious and political hot-spot – a fascinating but deeply troubled town, seeming to be constantly on the edge of combusting and taking the world with it. The following year, days before waves of Arab armies threw themselves at Israel in an attempt to annihilate it, the Jews attacked first. The Six Day War which followed left the City in Jewish hands, and led inevitably to the rise of today's militant Islam, aggressive Zionism and even fundamental Christianity – all of which seemed inconceivable in the 1960s. Most rational people thought then that all forms of religion were on the wane and would inevitably, probably during our lifetime, be replaced by some sort of global, liberal humanism, and that would cause all religious and sectarian squabbles to neatly dissolve. Forty years on, it seems we got that seriously wrong.

***

All the members of the Great Mediterranean Circumnavigation Expedition met up again in the Old City. Pat and Roger's Matchless, with our old sidecar attached, had made it. So had the Ford Prefect with Chris and Paul, but both vehicles were in a sorry state. Without a lot of expensive work, they seemed unlikely to get much further.

After telling each other how we all got there and what had happened since we last met, we wandered around Jerusalem's endless alleyways and cramped little streets, seeing for ourselves the places that were at the bedrock of so much of our culture – the sights endlessly re-imagined by generations of good, bad and indifferent painters and writers: The Way of the Cross; The Holy Sepulchre; The Garden of Gethsemane; The

Pool of Siloam; Herod's Garden and St Stephen's Gate, where the first Christian martyr had been used for target practice. Then further afield, across the surrounding countryside: to Bethlehem; Jericho, where we ate dates straight from the palms near the ancient walls; the Essene Scroll Caves and a ridiculous bobbing swim in the Dead Sea with diarrhoea-ravaged bottoms being savaged by the stinging brine and our thin little arms and legs sticking up helplessly out of the scummy water.

Everyone came to the Holy Land with expectations of what the great Biblical sights should look like, and our ideas were based mostly on the work of epic film set-designers. Ideally, we thought, these places should breathe historical authenticity – be practically unaltered since the Bronze Age or the First Century. But, sadly, their original appearance had been completely obscured or even obliterated by centuries of glorification, decoration and embellishment, alternating with neglect and destruction. The simple stone vault where the body of Jesus had supposedly been laid on the first Good Friday, had, through centuries of effort, been transformed into a smoky, crumbling Christian theme park. It felt completely divorced from the event it celebrated, with soaring arches, lamps, candles, icons and incense. It was surrounded on the outside by massive wooden buttresses to stop it falling over, and was the constant cause of squabbles between the various sects who shared responsibility for keeping it holy and upright.

General Gordon's Garden Tomb was much more to the polite English taste. The Hero of Khartoum had toured the Holy Land on his way to fight the Sudanese down the Nile. He was deeply troubled by the lack of restraint and taste in the Holy Sepulchre – God would surely not allow his son to be interred, even for a couple of days, in such vulgar circumstances. And he had a problem with the church's location – inside the defensive walls. The Bible states that crucifixions were performed outside the Town. Convincing evidence, he surmised, that these Orthodox-Christian Johnnies had got it all wrong. So he set himself the task of sorting things out and finding Christ's real crucifixion and burial sites.

Depending more on spiritual 'dowsing' than scholarly archeology, he wandered around outside the City Walls until he came upon a rocky escarpment near the Damascus Gate. This, he felt, had the theatrical bleakness of the real Golgotha. A short distance away, he discovered what he felt must have been a burial chamber cut into the side of the hill, complete with a grooved channel along which to roll a large stone and seal the entrance. To a mystic such as Gordon, the whole package was spiritually satisfying and had an air of authenticity about it. After his own death at the hands of the Mahdi in Khartoum, his Anglican sympathizers backed his hunch, purchased the land and turned it into a simple garden – a restrained, correct and Protestant place. And, despite the vagueness of its historical accuracy, so much more 'real' than the architectural monstrosity in the town.

The General had ignored the possibility that, when the Emperor Constantine's Mother, Helena, first chose that place as the sight of the crucifixion and burial, it may well have been outside the town's defences. The walls had then moved several times over the centuries, naturally enveloping Christianity's most precious relic within them…but strong belief, combined with wishful thinking, can overcome a lot of awkward logic.

FOURTEEN: *Petra*

Meanwhile, back in the Jerusalem of 1966, the members of our own little itinerant sect had a few of our own truths to come to terms with:

We were all short of money.

Most of us were a little homesick, though no one admitted it out loud.

The remaining two vehicles were not going to go much further, so there was little point in their owners paying shipping charges to get them around Israel and across to Egypt. Even if they got to North Africa, the chances of slogging all the way across the vast Saharan wastelands to Morocco were slim.

There was a strong rumour amongst other travellers that the Libyan border was closed because of political upheavals in Tripoli, and if we couldn't get through Libya then the rest of North Africa was unreachable without a very long sea voyage.

Most importantly, the camaraderie and desire to carry on travelling together had diminished. We had lived and journeyed with each other, in larger or smaller combinations, for many, many weeks and, I think, had grown a little tired of each other's company.

I can't remember any serious arguments or unpleasantness (though Mike and Steve had had a few clashes), but I remember a growing general irritation with my companions, and can safely assume that they felt the same about me. My relationship with Stephen had certainly worsened. What I once thought of as his admirable decisiveness and certainty, I now tended to interpret as bossiness. We were both aware that our long friendship had lost its warmth and had become a little brittle and fractious. It had been a gradual process – difficult to pinpoint when or why it happened.

Perhaps I had grown up a little, felt more self-reliant and was beginning to lose the need of my adolescent, only-child tendency to hang out with a more confident and outgoing friend.

And maybe we were all just beginning to tire of the whole business of constant travelling. It was obvious that Mike had had enough and wanted to get back to England, to Lois and to life as a married man.

However, before we all wended our separate ways home to Blighty, Pat and Roger suggested it would be fun to travel together for one last time – to the ancient city of Petra.

The legendary rose-red ruins lay two hundred miles to the south, across the Jordanian Desert. We all wanted to go there, but the Matchless and the Ford had neither enough seats nor enough life in them to take us. Then someone suggested that we all chip in a small amount of our remaining money and hire a vehicle from the Aziz Car Co. near Herod's Gate. They only had cars with four seats, and since we had teamed up with a young Danish bloke called Henning, there were exactly twice that number in our party. But the solution was simple: four of us would go to the office, hire the motor, then drive around the corner, where the other four would pile aboard.

The car was a Ford Corsair and Mr. Aziz's Agent rented it to us on production of my licence (not noticing that it was only valid for motorbikes), a sizeable deposit, a basic fee, and finally a mileage charge of about 7p per mile. As we were expecting to travel around four hundred miles, that would quickly mount up and become a problem...unless we could somehow avoid it.

There is some force among young men in groups that makes them do daft things – things that they mightn't do on their own. So when someone in the great crush of bodies in the back of the car suggested that we could disconnect the milometer, we just sat and thought how much money it would save – it would make the journey affordable. It didn't seem to cross anyone's mind that, as none of us had a valid licence and the car was significantly overloaded, adding fraud to the potential charge sheet was foolish. Or, if it did occur to anyone, they didn't speak up.

So, just south of Amman, on the desert highway, we pulled the Corsair off the road and I reached behind the dashboard and waggled the milometer cable while Roger and Mike crawled underneath to see where it connected. After a few minutes fiddling with a pair of pliers, the dirty deed was done and we were free of the mileage charge.

Paying less for the journey didn't improve the conditions inside the cabin. Eight people in a small saloon is uncomfortably cramped. Add to that forty-odd degrees of heat and a hot wind blowing handfuls of sand through the open windows and it's a recipe for extreme discomfort. Also, with the weight of all the bodies on the back wheels, the steering became alarmingly light and we drifted from side-to-side down the dead straight strip of tarmac across the desert. Only the driver's seat wasn't multi-occupied and so the chance for a turn at the wheel was argued over fiercely, with frequent stops for changeovers. The pauses between driving sessions got longer as we got hotter, until we were spending as much time by the roadside as in the car.

During one of these halts, I felt like escaping the crush and so walked out into the wilderness for about a mile – away from any sight and sound of the road, or my sweaty, short-tempered companions. I wanted to experience, for a moment or two, the isolation that T. E. Lawrence wrote about and loved.

Soon the only noise was the sand whispering around the boulders, and the only thing to see was a huge, broken, grey-beige expanse of rock, sand, blinding light and sharp, deep shadows. The Bedouin must have hundreds of words to describe what I was looking at, but to me it was just a lonely, vast nothingness – and distinctly scary. It was easy to imagine the panic of being lost and the tricks that the mind of an isolated traveller would play in such alien emptiness. I was glad to turn around, tramp back over the uneven ground and in a few minutes see the black road and the pointed nose of the Corsair again, with my friends milling around it. Despite feeling certain I would look terrific in those flowing Arab robes, I knew I wasn't the stuff that could lead a revolt in the desert.

Another few sessions of sweaty discomfort brought us to Wadi Musa, where we turned down a tiny dirt track towards Petra, parked the car and gratefully tumbled out.

In front of us rose a ragged cliff face, stretching away as far as we could see on either side. Directly ahead, it was split by a narrow crack, zig-zagging up the face. This was the 'Siq', the gateway to the city – a passageway through the cliffs that was so hard to see it had kept the city safe and secret for millenia. At the entrance were two forlorn Arabs holding the reins of a decrepit-looking bunch of donkeys and horses with drooping heads and ribcages like xylophones. We were offered the services of some of these creatures to take us through the gorge. Partly through pity for the beasts, but mainly because of the exorbitant price their owners demanded, we refused – after all it couldn't be that far.

It took nearly an hour to weave our way through the dark, narrow canyon. There were times when we could stretch out our arms and almost touch both walls – and the daylight was just visible a long way straight up. The sun never penetrated these depths, so, at first, after the sweatiness of the car, it was very pleasant. Then, after a time, we began to regret not being up in the saddle – especially after having to crush ourselves against the walls to allow a couple of Americans to push past us, swaying on the top of two of the same beasts we'd been offered - and looking both smug and rich. Our disgust was compounded when one of the donkeys tried to take a bite out of Roger's arm.

Eventually we could see a crooked line of blinding light ahead of us – and when our eyes adjusted; there was the magnificent rust-red frontage of Petra's most emblematic building: The Treasury. Carved out of the solid rock face, it towered over the American's donkeys tethered nearby, making them look like two tiny, neglected toys.

Petra is now a major stopping point on the tourist trail – one of 'The Places You Must See Before You Die' – and costs a small fortune in entrance fees. I gather it is surrounded by many good hotels, large coach parks and a constant crowd of visitors, shepherded by squadrons of guides and, I hope, a much better line in horse flesh. But in late August 1966 we paid nothing to get in, and those mounted Yanks and a French couple were the only other tourists we saw.

Apart from the horse-wranglers, there appeared to be only two other locals in residence: a young man with a Coca Cola stall, and a very old man sawing away on a one-string fiddle. His weedy tune whined and echoed around the bowl of cliffs, emphasising the emptiness of the place.

But despite the magnificent desolation, we were all a bit preoccupied. Our homesickness was biting that day. We squatted in a half-circle in the shade of the Treasury and talked, for a while, about the menu for our favourite Sunday lunch, English drizzle and, of course, beans on toast. I think we were becoming ready to turn for home. Finally we pulled ourselves together, took stock of our fabulous surroundings and went to explore 'the rose-red city, half as old as time'.

Unlike those English school-visit-ruins that are only a few rows of crumbling foundations and half a flying buttress, Petra required no leap of imagination to see how it must have looked as a thriving, living place. The Nabataean merchants who had built it were a rich and sophisticated bunch. They admired the building styles of the great classical civilisations around them, but instead of erecting their major buildings conventionally, block by block, their landscape gave them the novel and painstaking idea of carving intricate edifices out of the solid cliffs: "Here is a rock face, a hammer and a chisel – please chip away everything that doesn't look like an enormous Greek temple".

Petra had been rediscovered, as far as the West was concerned, by a Swiss explorer called Burckhardt in 1812. The locals had, of course, never mislaid it, but to European scholars and dreamers, it was a lost place of stories and fable, once owned by Cleopatra and made rich by the countless caravans that sheltered there on their way to the markets of Damascus. Following a severe earthquake in the fourth century, the trade routes gradually moved away – west to the sea and east towards Palmyra. Then, over a few generations, the Nabataean Arabs moved on and, being in such an isolated and secret place, it had quietly disappeared into ruin and legend.

We spent the remaining hours of that day scrambling over the red rocks and high up on the cliff ramparts, in and out of tombs and temples, between crumbled houses and what might have been the remains of shops or stables. When the sun began to redden and drop towards the hills, we started looking for nooks or crannies to sleep in that night. As I came out of one smelly hole, a coughing-snort startled me and I looked up the path above to see a camel train padding quietly by. On the lead animal was a single Bedouin youth, who half-turned in his saddle to look down at me. Two young men, completely alien to each other, separated by chasms of culture, language and beliefs, grinned at each other briefly, then turned back to get on with our lives.

Over the next ten hours, with no sleeping bags or means to make a fire, we discovered what I expect the camel driver knew very well: desert nights can get very cold. Soon after dawn it was good to feel the early sun warming our bones and coaxing the blood back into our fingers and toes, as we made our way down from our stony bedrooms, through the chasm and back to the Ford Corsair.

The desert road was busier that day. Several times we had to veer sharply off the tarmac and into the sandy, rock-strewn landscape, away from large Lorries roaring down the dead centre of the narrow strip towards us. How we avoided tyre-bursts, or even turning over on the rough ground, is a tribute to whichever factories the little car and its tyres came from.

Several sweaty, bouncing hours later found us safely back near the outskirts of Amman. Time to re-connect the milometer. Roger scrambled underneath the engine, found the loose cable and screwed it home. We drove on, but several miles later, the gauge hadn't shown a change. Someone else repeated the process – no miles registered. We tried again and again, but couldn't make the thing count the distance. We were in trouble. No one was going believe that the counter had just stopped working. Each of us began to imagine the penalty and punishment that the car hire people might try to land us with, and what we might say to side-step the results of our idiocy. Swearing innocence and accusing Ford of sloppy manufacture seemed an unbelievable alibi, even to naive optimists like us.

Halfway between Amman and Jerusalem, twenty miles from Herod's Gate, we were all silently contemplating our fate – particularly the four of us who had done the hiring and had to return the vehicle. Then suddenly, from the back seat, Henning yelled "IT IS VORKING!" Heads banged together as we all tried to see the console. He was right – the numbers were slowly sliding upwards from 7 to 8. The cable core had miraculously become aligned to the cogs below and clicked home. The milometer was functioning and our bacon was saved. The relief was enormous – we stopped the car and all did a little air-punching dance on the pavement, and I made a silent promise to myself never to do anything as silly as that again on this journey…a vow I had forgotten well within a week.

The Agent at Aziz's emporium raised his eyebrow when he calculated our mileage charge. "It appears you have only travelled a small distance," he mused. "But the car is so dusty…inside and out." He looked each of us squarely in the eye, and together we all shrugged, gave him faintly desperate, beatific smiles, picked up our deposit and sidled out of the door.

FIFTEEN: *The End of the Fellowship*

It was time to disband the travelling circus and, by one means or another, begin our journeys home. No one wanted to re-trace the overland route we'd followed to get to Jerusalem – that was a depressing prospect, and a very, very long way. The best alternatives involved finding some way to get across the Mediterranean and into southern Europe: to Greece, Italy, or even far away France. Which route each traveller chose depended partly on how quickly they wanted to get back, but primarily on how much cash they had.

Throughout the life of the bike, we three on TOF 80 had contributed equally towards paying for food, petrol and other daily expenses – and after it had gone, we'd paid our way individually. However, I don't think any of us discussed how much money was stashed in the foul depths of each rucksack. Perhaps the most equable thing would have been to pool all our remaining resources, then divide it equally amongst the three, or even all seven. Thereby making everyone's chances on the return trip equal. But our brotherly-love must have evaporated a little by then, because it was never even discussed. And so individually, or with a companion, for the first time since leaving England, we each began to make different plans.

I have no memory of how much money I had set off with from Birmingham in June, or how much was left by the time I reviewed my options in the seedy dormitory in Jerusalem. But because of my parent's gift of the folded tenner, and because I had been at work earning wages for a few years (Blomberg/Beaman were paying me about £11 a week), I had a bit more cash than my student friends – just enough for me to risk pushing on alone to Egypt. It was a scary prospect, to make my own way into a very foreign place without the security of my dependable companions, but to be so near the Valley of the Kings and then to turn away seemed a bit weedy. (No one could have known then that in a few decades it would be just a three-hour flight away from Heathrow, and that people would pop over for a long weekend and a quick gawp at a tomb or temple).

When I voiced my idea, in a half-baked, thinking-out-loud way, all my friends insisted that, if they were in my sandals, they would definitely journey on to see the great things down the Nile. Surely, they said, I would never forgive myself if I didn't do it. It would be a real disappointment to scurry back home whilst there were a few quid left in my rucksack.

After a moment or two of paranoia: they all seemed very keen that I should disappear over the horizon alone. I became convinced and confident: everything would be alright; it would be fine travelling completely solo; nothing to be nervous of; just another few weeks on the road; and with marvellous things to see. A great end to the adventure.

Later, however, in the thick, stuffy darkness of the dormitory, I spent the inevitable sleepless hours imagining all the horrors and awfulness waiting for me. There would be no one to pick up the pieces and help me cope with problems, and how would I deal with constant loneliness? Was there much point in being somewhere wonderful if there was no one to share it with?

But, by then, it would have been far too humiliating to chicken out, admit my misgivings and stick with the crowd. It was bravado, not bravery, that wrenched me from the others and set me off alone.

Early next morning, I shuffled reluctantly along the row of creaky single beds and said my farewells. We all wished each other goodbye and good luck, but considering how interdependent we had been over the previous months, there was surprisingly little emotion in the parting. It may be that, in the mid-60s, we were still rather British and understated – not yet given to the ebullient shows of emotion which now seem part of our common currency. Plus, I imagine everyone else had had their own night of worries as to how they were going to get home safely, and that led to a degree of introspection which made us all subdued. Whatever the reasons, almost overnight, we seemed to have become a collection of individuals, instead of a group with a single aim.

Initially, all six of my ex-fellow travellers were heading together through the Mandelbaum Gate to the nearest harbours in Israel, looking for the cheapest boats going anywhere in Europe. But a Jewish stamp in my passport would make my visit to the Land of the Pharaohs impossible, so I had to travel the two-hundred miles back to the Beirut dockside to buy a passage for Alexandria.

Steve walked with me to the Jerusalem walls and we smiled and shook hands. Then, feeling miserably alone and a quite scared, I climbed onto the same ancient bus that had brought us here, struggled to a window seat and, as it slowly pulled away, waved through the filthy glass at the diminishing figure of my old friend.

The temptation to shout "Stop the bus! Forget Egypt! I'll stick with you guys!" was almost irresistible, but then the bus driver savaged a gear and we gathered speed, sending up a cloud of dust that quickly hid the Old City and my Mediterranean Circumnavigation companions for good. Next stop: Amman and the Lebanese highway – as a solitary traveller.

SIXTEEN: *M.S. Messalia*

Forty-eight hours later, in Beirut and trying to ignore the aching loneliness in my gut, my first stop was at the kiosk of a money-changer near the docks to do a bit of illegal trading. Egypt had a 'closed currency', which meant no one was permitted to export or import its money into or out of the country. However, I'd been told, by some other occupants of the hostel in Jerusalem, that 'everyone' bought Egyptian Pounds in Lebanon at amazing exchange rates, simply because it was useless paper beyond its own borders. The speculators purchased it at silly prices, primarily from Egyptians who came over to trade in Beirut and had no access to foreign money. These dealers tacked on their mark-up and were still able to offer it at tempting rates to anyone prepared to smuggle it back into Egypt.

Sure enough, they were almost giving Egyptian currency away. I was offered more than twice the rate that could be expected in a bank in Cairo, so I changed half of my Sterling into wodges of crumpled, grubby notes. If my gamble paid off I could travel around Egypt for a while and then, at my port of exit, change the money back into British Pounds, making enough profit from the transaction to get home. Unfortunately, I hadn't taken into account my poor abilities with arithmetic, or remembered my silent promise, after the car fiasco, to stick to the straight and narrow.

Next I went to a Greek shipping office and, with some of my remaining Sterling, bought a deck passage on the MS Messalia, which was leaving that afternoon and calling into Port Said and Alexandria the next day.

One of the cheapest ways to travel the Mediterranean is on the open deck of one of the hundreds of small tramp steamers that plough backwards and forwards in every direction. No accommodation or shelter is provided, just whatever space you can find on the metal deck-plates. Fortunately, in late August, storms were unlikely and we were fairly certain of warm days and dry nights.

Messalia was a small rust-bucket that spent its long but unremarkable life chugging backwards and forwards across these waters, shifting anything or anybody from one port to another. It had a single, crooked smokestack and a worn and noisy engine, which reminded me fondly of TOF 80, and was indistinguishable from a million other humble vessels that had made the same journeys ever since the time of the Phoenicians. Time and technology had changed the look of these ships, but their purpose remained exactly the same.

As I climbed up the gangplank and found myself a spot on the open deck amongst a large crowd of Lebanese and Egyptians, it was instantly obvious there would be no invitation to the Captain's table for any of us that night. Most of my fellow passengers were in big family groups and carried all sorts of goods bought in the Beirut Souks. Everyone seemed very friendly, but I was constantly warned, in broken English and mime, to carefully guard my belongings. They all seemed to suggest, with knowing forefinger taps on the sides of their noses, that the boat was mostly exporting villains.

A large and entrepreneurial woman swathed in black set up a food stall near the stern and I was able to buy flatbread and some tomatoes. Then, as both Lebanon and the sun disappeared behind the horizon, I tried to settle down in my sleeping bag and get some rest. Unfortunately, through the hours of darkness, the noise from the engines and my fellow passengers rose and fell like the sea – sudden laughter, children crying, shouted arguments and plenty of snoring. Occasionally a crew-member would burst out from some door or hatchway and stumble his way across the moving deck and into the prone bodies, causing loud complaints from the people he trod on. Not a great night's sleep, but the stars were spectacular.

Soon after dawn the Messalia edged into the harbour at Port Said, where some of my fellow deck passengers disembarked and were replaced by a few new faces, including one European. He spotted me, strolled across towards my little spot and, in excellent English, introduced himself as Kurt and said he was heading for Cairo. Despite being German, he was either ignorant of the result of the World Cup, or didn't care, so was able to talk to a Brit.

The striking thing about Kurt's appearance was his complete lack of hair – nothing on his head at all, no eyelashes, eyebrows or hint of a beard and moustache. When listening to him, it was difficult not to be distracted and find one's gaze straying across his face in search of some hint of follicles. He was presumably used to this, because he soon explained that his condition was caused by some childhood illness. I assured him that I had barely noticed. He might have raised an eyebrow at that, but who could tell?

As the Messalia chugged its way across the mouth of the Nile Delta and along the North African coast, we passed the time by telling each other how we had got there. He came from Bavaria and wanted to do a post-graduate course in Egyptology at Heidelberg and thought a visit to the great Pharaohic museums would improve his chances of acceptance. So he had taken a train to Marseille and a boat to Port Said, and then had had problems travelling overland to Cairo, so decided to take the sea route instead.

Finally we went through the ritual of exchanging books – a regular routine amongst the itinerant classes.

Paperbacks were one of the few sources of distraction during hours of travelling and nights in miserable hostels, and so were precious, almost having the same currency value as 'snout' does for prisoners.

I gave him a tattered Agatha Christie I'd swapped in Jerusalem, and he presented me with Mary McArthy's *The Group*, telling me that it was a woman's book, but better than nothing. He was right. I may not have been its intended demographic, but it was something new to read and therefore a real treat. Over the next week I read it from cover-to-cover.

In the late afternoon the Messalia tied up alongside the dock in Alexandria, and amongst the throng of our fellow passengers, Kurt and I made our way to the customs-shed. There we were told to fill in all the usual forms, plus a statement of how much foreign currency we were bringing into the country. I filled in the exact amount of Sterling that I had left, just in case I was asked to prove it, whilst being nervously aware that I had more than twice that amount in smuggled Egyptian notes at the bottom of my rucksack. Fortunately none of the officials seemed inclined to search my seedy baggage, and I was handed a form that would allow me to exchange any unspent Egyptian pounds back into proper money when leaving the country. With visas checked and passports stamped, we wandered through the dock gates, into the Land of the Pharaohs to look for a Youth Hostel.

Kurt and I were getting on perfectly well, and were quite glad of each other's company, so we agreed to travel together as far as Cairo, do the main sights and the Egyptology museum, where many of Howard Carter's finds from Tutankhamen's tomb, including the great, gold funerary mask, were on show, and then go our separate ways. He would head back to Europe and his interview at Heidelberg, and I intended to carry on down the Nile to see Luxor, Karnak and the Valley of the Kings.

Within the week we had seen most of what Cairo's museums had to offer – had spent many hours nosing around the stuff left by long-dead people. Finally, on our last day together, we went to Giza, a few miles out of the City, and spent an expensive morning plodding along, on the back of a pair of camels, looking at the Pyramids. I couldn't really afford a pricey treat like that, but Kurt insisted that it was a fine old tradition – one of the necessary and inevitable things that visitors to Egypt had to do. There must be thousands of almost-identical sepia prints, colour slides and even Facebook entries showing slightly-tense tourists – General Gordon, Winston Churchill and Noel Coward amongst them – astride their disdainful mounts, with the Sphinx and Pyramids in the background. I liked the idea of being part of that crowd, so I paid the inflated fee, was introduced to my mount, and climbed aboard her fringed and tasseled saddle.

After our bouncing, lolloping ride around the great monuments, the rest of the day was spent less expensively: scrambling, up and over the huge stone blocks that make up the Great Pyramid, and creeping through the dark, claustrophobic passageways leading to Cheops's burial chamber. I tried to climb up the outside, to the apex of the triangle, four-hundred-and-eighty feet high, but a combination of heat, tiredness and vertigo defeated me long before I'd got a quarter of the way up.

SEVENTEEN: *Down the Nile*

Despite the Pyramids and the dusty wonders in the Museum of Antiquities – and my discovery of food barrows in the street selling a cheap and quite tasty bean stew called 'Foul' – Cairo, that September, was a hot, smelly and chaotic place. It seemed to be full of aggressive spivs trying to sell me bits of tourist tat at silly prices.

Hawkers made life difficult for visitors to Egypt. In all the big cities of the Middle-East, we had become used to men hissing at us from dark doorways with offers of money-changing, souvenirs, or even occasionally their sisters, but here the frequency of 'shopping opportunities' became an overwhelming flood. The sales pitch was almost always the same: they had just made a precious 'find' in their garden, or while walking in the desert, whether it was a string of ancient beads, a scarab, or a little stone votive figure of a pharaoh. And, because I was a man of taste, they would allow me first refusal of this little treasure. Usually the paint was barely dry on the priceless antique, and the mould lines stuck up like tram tracks.

Having got rid of one desperate, pushy and eventually aggressive salesman, he was instantly replaced by two others. It was impossible to walk the streets and see anything beyond the crappy things shoved under your nose, to ignore the constant pleading, pulling and poking, or eventually keep an even temper.

So I wasn't sorry to be waiting for the Night Train that ran south to Luxor and Upper Egypt. But as I stood on the platform with a third-class ticket tucked in my pocket, I noticed that all the people around me were women and older men. Groups of younger males were skulking about further down the line in the direction the train would approach from, and when the Nile Express finally nosed towards us, they scrambled and leapt through the open doors and windows, filling the cheaper compartments before the rest of us got a foot onboard. It was like the mayhem outside Harrods on the first day of the January Sales. By the time I got into a third-class carriage, all the slatted wooden benches were crammed and the young queue-jumpers were even lying languidly across the luggage racks overhead. The women and oldies quickly crammed themselves onto the floor between the seats, leaving me perched on my rucksack and jammed up against the lavatory partition.

The train's progress along the Nile Valley was intermittent: sometimes smooth and fast, then suddenly grinding to a clanking, juddering halt. I unsuccessfully tried to snooze through the long night hours, but by the time the first hint of dawn crept into the carriage, I was suffering from lack of sleep and my temper was frayed. It was clear that most of my fellow passengers didn't want me there on their floor space. When I smiled and nodded no one responded, and I was often jostled or pushed by people on their way to visit the hole in the floor behind my clapboard backrest.

My temper finally snapped when a peddler carrying bottles of Coke in a tin bucket slopped water all over my legs and feet. He did it casually and then grinned at the other passengers. Suddenly my tiredness, bad diet, grinding bowels and resentment at all Egyptian hawkers surfaced. I leapt up, swore loudly and pushed him away. He pushed back and we were soon locked together, shouting into each other's faces and shoving ineffectually, unable to move or hit out in the crush, or even understand each other's insults. Then the bucket went over and water gushed across the dusty floor, and instantly everyone was on their feet shouting and grabbing at me. I think I was about to be ejected out of the carriage door and onto the tracks, but fortunately, before I found myself alone on the banks of the Nile in a crumpled heap, the Conductor pushed his way through the mob, shouted at everyone, then grabbed me and my rucksack and shoved us both into the concertina section between carriages.

He explained that tourists didn't belong in third-class. They were resented by the very poor people who normally used it. We were seen as rich and therefore should be on the soft seats up the train. I produced my ticket to prove I had been in the right place, but that was waved away, and he led me along the train to the tranquility of a second-class compartment. He held out his hand and I took the hint and dropped a donation into it before settling down, gratefully, onto the leatherette seats. Before he left he told me that, on my return journey back to Cairo, I was also to travel second – just slip the Conductor a tip and he would be happy to turn a blind eye to anything my ticket stated. It seemed that a lot of official business was done like that in Egypt.

The last bit of the journey was spent dozing and talking to a schoolteacher from Aswan. A pleasant contrast to being mobbed. My new companion was an amateur violinist and, during our chat, he told me how difficult it was to get fiddle strings in his small town. He asked if I would send him a set from England and I promised I would - and put the slip of paper with his address on it into my bag.

It was about seven in the morning when the train pulled into Luxor. I climbed down and started to look for the Youth Hostel. There was no information kiosk or town map in the station, and Steve's mental sat nav was several hundred miles to the north. So asking passers-by seemed the only alternative.

I had just thanked the last of a line of shouldershruggers who either didn't understand the question or had no idea where the place was, when the early-morning sun was blocked out by a huge man in a tight, dark suit, tapping me on the shoulder. "Get in car," he rumbled and jerked his thumb towards a large, black Mercedes. Without waiting for my response, he picked up my heavy rucksack between his finger and thumb, put his other enormous paw in the middle of my back and propelled me towards the kerb. Moments later I was perched nervously on a fold-down seat, opposite my abductor and his equally-large doppelganger who sat, like a pair of oversized bookends, on the back seat. Stuck between them was a small, elderly man in full Arab dress, smoking a Turkish cigarette. All three of them wore impenetrable sunglasses, so I had no idea what they were thinking or intending to do with me. The first man leaned forward, tapped the glass screen behind me and the car glided away from the station forecourt. I smiled nervously and asked where we were going. The two heavies looked out of the windows and the Man in the Middle nodded seriously and patted me on the knee, but didn't reply. I hoped that meant that their grasp of English was as good as my Arabic.

I spent the next few minutes looking out at the dusty, run-down streets zipping past and wondering if I was in some sort of fix, then suddenly we stopped. The first Heavy jerked his thumb again and said "Yudd Hossel". I looked up and there on the corner of the building opposite was the familiar YHA triangle. They weren't arresting, molesting or kidnapping me – just giving me a lift.

After relieved smiles and thanks from me, and expressionless nods in return, I climbed out, retrieved my bag, then went into the Hostel to find a bed and have a nap. It had been an eventful, restless journey from Cairo to Luxor and I was worn out.

Around noon I was feeling a bit livelier, so I decided to walk down to the banks of the Nile. After more than three months of summer travel in a southerly direction, I thought I was acclimatised to hot weather. But stepping out from the shade of the Hostel doorway, with the midday sun directly overhead, was like falling into a baker's oven. The September heat was intense and the air felt hot and thick in my lungs. Noel Coward's 'Mad dogs and Englishmen' suddenly sounded less like a comic song and more like factual reporting.

Fortunately the riverbank wasn't far, so I sweated and wheezed my way to it and was able to find some shade under a palm tree at the water's edge, and dangle my feet in the tepid, soupy water.

A little further down the bank from where I was sitting, a fisherman walked into the river carrying a vast triangular net supported on two thin, springy poles. He began to lower and raise it into the flow, and diamonds of light sparkled and bounced off the fine mesh. Just beyond him two elegant feluccas, with their triangular sails filled by the warm breeze, swept along the great river against the backdrop of the lush, green banks opposite. Across the water, I could just see a small, harnessed donkey walking slowly round in circles, operating an ancient wooden machine that pulled river water into the fields...a timeless and very beautiful scene. The difficulties of the train journey diminished. This was what I'd come all that way for. It was one of those perfect moments that are rare on most journeys, but the main reason for making all the effort. My only regrets were that there was no one with me to share it, and I'd left the camera at the hostel.

Back in the YHA dormitory, I was given two pieces of good advice by a Swede in the next bed. He'd been there for a week and so had an air of experience and authority:

1: Don't get any part of your anatomy in the Nile. Even paddling in it risked infection from the Bilharzia bug. This little horror would burrow through your skin and keep nibbling its way through your limbs until it got to your vitals. Having just returned from dipping my feet in the river, I immediately – and for sometime after – inspected every inch of them carefully. (Forty years on, I think I got away with it.)

2: Hire a push-bike to speed up travel between the ruins - and start sightseeing at dawn. Then be back indoors by eleven-thirty - and don't go out again till late-afternoon. Being in the shade during the hottest hours wasn't just a siesta, more an act of self-preservation.

Over the next week, I was up before the sun and down to the Town Square to pay a few piastres for the hire of an upright, gearless bicycle. Then I would peddle away on the old wreck to the ruins of Karnak on the East Bank. Or, if I wanted to see the tombs and temples of Western Thebes, a grizzled, old ferryman in a wooden boat would row me and my wheels across the river.

I think part of my lifelong dislike of cycling stems from the sweaty, straining sessions between those magnificent ruins – trying to keep the old boneshaker from upending me onto the stony paths. But climbing off the lumpy saddle and standing in the Valley of the Kings, or amongst the toppled stones of the Ramesseum, or beneath the Colossi of Memnon, did make the effort more than worthwhile.

EIGHTEEN: *Northwards*

Eventually even the most wonderful and evocative of places begins to pall, especially when you're vaguely homesick and extremely skint. For a while I thought about continuing south to Aswan and Lake Nasser, but then admitted to myself that I'd had enough. I was trekked-out and it was time to follow my friends' example and head home.

The next day my third-class ticket, plus a small bribe, got me a seat in second on the Cairo train. A bus took me to the northern outskirts of the capital, and then a lorry and finally a delivery van to the port of Alexandria.

Throughout the two days it took to reach the coast I had been contemplating, with increasing dread, changing what was left of my smuggled Egyptian money back into Sterling. The cut-price currency scam had seemed an easy money-making scheme when the bloke in Jerusalem had described it, and even seemed reasonable at the exchange-booth in Beirut. But now I had to face Egyptian Officialdom, and that was where the whole thing could seriously unravel.

Since arriving in the country, I had enjoyed camel rides, train journeys, visits to temples and tombs and daily plates of 'Foul', all bought using the illegally-obtained currency – and I still had about half of it left. That small profit, plus my original tiny stash of Sterling, was desperately needed to get me across Europe, so I was hoping that the bank officials wouldn't take any notice of dodgy details – just wave it all through and pay me my money.

If, on the other hand, it all went wrong and my little scheme was blown, currency-smuggling was a criminal offence and I could end up doing a spell in an Egyptian clink. I had heard enough about the prison conditions in the Middle East and the habits of the inmates to be very nervous.

In the late afternoon I arrived at the Bank, shuffled around in the hit-and-miss fashion that the Egyptians call queuing, and was eventually called through into a small kiosk. Sitting at the other side of the desk was a thin, middle-aged man with silver-grey hair and a large, black moustache. Without looking up, he held out a hand for the claim form, my passport and the money I wished to exchange. He counted the banknotes, looked at the forms, counted again, then sat back and finally looked at me. "How do you account for the fact that you have been in our country for almost three weeks, and yet appear to have spent virtually no money?"

My limitations as a competent con man immediately showed. I blushed furiously and began to sweat, then stammered "I have been staying with a friend". He paused, frowned, then asked for details, and in a moment of either panic or inspiration, I produced the slip of paper showing the address given to me by my violin-playing companion on the Luxor train.

"This will all need further investigation," he said. "I shall retain your passport and these documents, and tomorrow morning at nine o'clock you must return. Come back into this office, then I shall tell you how we will proceed. Good evening *Mr.* Fisher".

Good evening indeed…what followed was amongst the worst nights of my life.

Sixteen sleepless, sweating, pacing, tossing-and-turning hours later, and wearing my tidiest shirt, I called into a barber's shop to have a proper shave. For some reason I thought that looking as smart as possible might count in my favour at the Bank: "Surely this elegant young Englishman cannot be a criminal?"

I then bought stamps for two letters written during

the long night hours – one for my parents and one for Janet, telling them that I was unfortunately delayed in Egypt, and whilst they mustn't worry, it might be wise to get in touch with the British Consulate for news. I gambled on being able to post them before I was led away in chains.

The bronze bank doors were being swung open by a Commissionaire in the uniform of a South-American Field-Marshal as I arrived, and I was told to wait in the main hall. Eventually my tormentor came to the doorway of his little kiosk and ushered me in. The door was shut and he sat at his desk. There was no other chair, so I was left standing.

After a long pause, he said "I am aware of what you have done". Another, much longer pause. My shirt began to go wet around the armpits and I could feel runnels of sweat trickling from my hairline.

"However (another pause) the sums involved are too small to warrant carrying the matter further. So I will exchange your currency and ask you to leave Egypt as soon as is convenient".

I must have gone chalky-white with relief, because he almost looked concerned for a moment. He didn't want an unconscious smuggler littering up his tiles. After I'd regained some composure, he produced from a desk drawer a small bundle of Sterling. He counted out three tiny piles, then lent back in his chair.

"In order to compensate the Bank for its trouble, I have decided to withhold an amount...for expenses". With that, he swept up two of the piles and put them back in his drawer. After signing a form stating that I had received the full amount, grabbing my passport and stuffing the third pile of cash in my pocket, I muttered thanks and was out of his den and the Bank like a self-propelled grenade.

It was a slick and well-practiced sting, though,

involving such a tiny amount of money, I suspect he was just keeping his hand in. He had started by first letting me know, the previous afternoon, that my misdemeanor was discovered, and then left me to dangle overnight, knowing that my imagination would soften me up. Finally, the next day, he offered me a way out – for a price. Even leaving me a third of the money was smart – it made sure I didn't make a fuss. I suspect his managers had no knowledge of what had gone on in that tiny room, and would never see anything of the small stash of notes he'd confiscated. However, I was profoundly grateful to have met a casual crook, rather than an honest avenging official. It's possible he also saw himself as a counsellor who showed me what little potential I had as a smuggler and criminal mastermind, and he was therefore entitled to an appropriate fee. Forty years on, I still think it was good value.

And thank goodness the panic-letters to my parents and girlfriend hadn't been posted in advance. I took them out from my pocket and, with still trembling fingers, ripped them up. Then, within an hour, I was at the Hellenic Shipping Line offices, booking a deck passage out of North Africa and away from the man with the moustache.

NINETEEN: *See Naples and Starve*

The next morning, confused by Arabic signs and my topographic inadequacies, I got hopelessly lost on my way to the harbour, and after running from berth to berth, trying to find the right boat, I arrived just as the crew were preparing to raise the gangplank. In my panic I hadn't made time for breakfast or to buy food for the crossing, but I trusted that there would be a café or restaurant onboard – or at least another little old lady setting up a makeshift market-stall to sell bread and fruit.

SS. Media belonged to the same Greek company as the Messalia, which had brought me to Egypt. It was a little larger, a trifle younger, but only slightly less decrepit. Though its engines were noticeably quieter, there was still a fair amount of rust and dirt everywhere. As well as us poor people squatting over its fore-decks, it also boasted three or four cabins at the stern – for a better class of traveller. I assume these people were given meals in their cabins by a steward, or fed in a saloon below decks, because there was no food openly for sale anywhere – no café and no old lady with a stall.

Ahead was a long crossing of the Med: past Crete, through the Cycladian Islands, a stop for a few hours at the quayside of Piraeus near Athens, then west through the Corinth Canal and across the Ionian Sea into Italian waters. Finally, through the Straits of Messina, between Sicily and the toe of Italy, past Capri and the ruins of Pompeii, before eventually docking at Naples...

It was the sort of voyage that people on cruise ships pay good money for – but for them, on a vessel oozing with bars and restaurants, it's almost impossible not to overindulge. My outlook, on SS. Media, was five days of starvation…twelve-hundred hungry miles.

As Alexandria slowly disappeared below the horizon, I watched with envy as groups of fellow passengers spread out picnics, made mint tea and wonderful smelling coffee on small camping stoves and poured out glasses of wine for each other. Eventually they finished stuffing themselves and sat back, belching and smiling with contentment. None of them gave a glance at the miserable creature with big eyes and a rumbling stomach sitting nearby. At least I could have a drink: there was a tap over a drain nearby for the use of the deck-people, though the water tasted rusty and stale.

When darkness fell, several of the crew began to raise a large, rectangular white sheet from a mast in the middle of the decks. It was soon obvious that this was a cinema screen and my mood lightened. A bit of entertainment was just what I needed to take my mind off the emptiness inside me. However, when it was finally tied off, the screen had been carefully angled so that it was only properly visible from the stern cabins. The cabin occupants then brought out deckchairs and sat around, chatting with each other and sipping cool drinks from long, ice-filled glasses. Eventually, after a lot of faffing by one of the crew, the projector fired up and a black-and-white film flickered onto the screen. It might have been a French 'Film Noir' or an American thriller, but had been dubbed into another tongue, possibly Greek, Turkish or Arabic. Whichever it was, from my very acute angle it was frustratingly invisible and totally incomprehensible.

In a rotten mood and very hungry, I lay down in my sleeping bag on the deck-plates and drifted into a miserable, resentful sleep, feeling like a fully-fledged member of the undeserving poor.

In the early hours, the wind got up and a heavy sea

began to toss our little boat around. Everyone was woken by the motion, and quite a few of my neighbours lost their evening meals over the side. But, although the sounds of retching and groaning made me feel a little queasy, I had nothing in my stomach and so was at least able to indulge in petty feelings of 'serves 'em right for eating'.

The next morning, as the Media chugged past Crete and skirted alongside the islands of the Cyclades, the sea became calm again and we spent all the daylight hours cruising across a rich blue millpond. Then later, when the sun dropped towards the western horizon, the sky turned scarlet and the water into Homer's 'Wine Dark Sea'. With a full stomach I would have been enthralled.

It was past midnight when we docked at Piraeus near Athens, and then we all had the pleasure of a few hours sleep on a steady deck, securely tied up to the Greek mainland.

I woke early the next morning full of hope. Before the boat left at nine a.m. I thought there was a chance to go ashore and find a food store or marketplace to buy something delicious and filling. But when I approached the dock gates, the guard reasonably reminded me that I couldn't just stroll into Greece for half-an-hour, do some shopping and stroll out again. It was necessary to go through Customs and Passport Control, introduce myself properly to the Authorities and fill in all the usual forms.

Then, having got beyond the bureaucracy and the gates, I would have to wander the streets, beyond the mass of cranes, warehouses and stores that surround any dockside, until I found more conventional shopping streets in which hopefully I could locate a Bank, and, if they were open that early, go through the long-winded process of changing a tiny amount of Sterling into

Drachmas. Finally, I needed to find a shop selling something that I could afford and even hopefully enjoy. Walking everywhere was my only option, because, as I didn't speak Greek, hiring and giving directions to a taxi would be fraught with potential misunderstanding and cost Drachmas I didn't yet possess.

Would there be time to do all that before the S.S. Media left her berth? Or would I get hopelessly lost again, only arriving back at the quayside to watch as it pulled away for Italy and home without me? As I contemplated all the problems, a miserable lethargy came over me and I eventually resigned myself to giving up, skulking back onboard and being hungry until Naples. It was apathetic, but I was too tired and hungry to care by then. So, defeated and feeling very sorry for myself, I crept back to my spot on the deck until it was time for the boat to pull away.

Just to rub salt – and a handful of chopped herbs – into my wounds, a few hours out of Piraeus all of my neighbours on deck began to prepare for their next meal. Stoves were lit, out came the table cloths again, and baskets were rifled for food.

I must have been unconsciously transfixed by the lunch preparations of the family nearest to me – when they settled down to eat, with the movement of their hands taking food up to their mouths, then the steady chewing of their jaws – because, after a while, a woman in the group noticed my fascination and whispered to a small boy sitting in their circle. He uncrossed his legs, and with a very serious face, got up and walked over to me, holding out a hard-boiled egg. I held up my hands in apology for my ogling of their food, but the group waved away my embarrassment and I gratefully took it.

After I'd peeled it and looked lovingly at its unblemished perfection for a moment or two, I ate it very, very slowly. Forty years on, I can still taste the smooth, firm white and the crumbly yolk. Having seen me then reverently pick up and eat every tiny morsel that had fallen into my lap, they must have realised how grateful (and ravenous) I was, because a little while later the same boy brought me a small piece of bread. After that, the word seemed to have got around, because, most mealtimes, several of the other eating-clubs around the deck sent across small morsels to the pathetic Englishman. These people were poor, but they shared what they were carefully rationing for the whole voyage with a young bloke they didn't know at all.

So with a tiny bit of food in my belly, I began to enjoy the voyage a little more. It was, for instance, impossible not to be impressed by the Corinth Canal. It seemed just wide enough for S.S. Media to squeeze through and its almost vertical walls towered over our tallest mast. These artificial cliffs had been chiselled and blasted through the four miles of rock which once joined mainland Europe to the Peloponnese, but sadly, despite all the painstaking civil engineering and massive effort, the canal proved to be a white elephant: often closed because of landslips from its steep sides, and not wide enough to allow the much larger ocean-going ships of the twentieth century to sail through. But onboard a small vessel like ours it was a great spectacle. A group of tiny figures on the iron bridge that crossed the gulf at the halfway point shouted greetings down to us as we passed below them, and we all waved and cheered back.

After emerging from the canal, a slow chug through the rest of the Gulf of Corinth took all day, so it was dark before we passed between the islands of Cephalonia and Zakinthos and reached the open waters of the Ionian Sea. Another day took us across into Italian waters, and during that night we curved around the toe of Italy, through the Straits of Messina and were on the home run to Napoli.

Five long days after leaving Alexandria, SS.Media docked and I said goodbye and a last thank you to all the people who, during the voyage, had just about kept me from starvation. Then we all shuffled down the gangplank onto European soil, and then through the fifteenth customs-post of my journey.

Before the ink had dried on the new stamp in my passport, I was through the dock gates, had exchanged some Sterling into Lire, and was heading for the nearest eating place, intending to have a slap-up feast of fine Italian food. It had been a constant promise to myself from the very first hours onboard the boat, and I had dreamt incessantly of rich tomato sauce, crusty bread, pizza and sweet puddings.

In the nearest cheap-looking workman's café I spent several minutes salivating over the promises on the menu, and then ordered a bowl of minestrone as a starter. Sadly, from the first rich spoonful of vegetables, pasta and broth, it became apparent that my eyes were much bigger than my belly. After days of emptiness on the boat (and a very hit-and-miss diet before that), my capacity had shrunk to almost nothing. After less than half a bowl, I was on the edge of feeling bloated and sick, so I reluctantly paid up and went off to find somewhere to kip. The next morning would be soon enough to try a slower and gentler re-introduction to the business of eating.

I slept on a wooden park bench near the Castel Nuovo, where, four years before, to celebrate my eighteenth birthday, Steve and I had gone to see 'Madam Butterfly'. The bench was too short, but, unlike the deck of the Media, it stayed still all night. And the local police didn't wake me to check my papers and move me on until it was almost dawn.

TWENTY: *Home Run*

Hitching up through Italy was a long, slow slog. It started well, when I found a local bus which terminated in the northern suburbs of Naples, near the Autostrada. Then, almost as soon as I had stuck out my thumb, a battered Fiat 500 stopped. It was driven by a young teacher who was keen to practice his English, and he took me right into Rome, to the Piazza outside the Central Railway Station. There, after a cheap meal, I found another bench for the night – too short and hard for comfort again, but this time a striking piece of Modernist marble on one of the station platforms. Unfortunately throughout the night the Polizia di Roma were far more persistent than their Neapolitan comrades, prodding me incessantly with their night sticks and insisting that I must sit up and keep both feet on the ground. Eventually, in the early hours, the shifts must have changed and they left me alone, until I was disturbed by the first commuters invading my bedroom on suburban trains, slamming their carriage doors and shouting incomprehensible conversations at each other. Soon they wanted to share my bench, so, grudgingly, I gave up and moved on.

Before the sun became too hot, I walked across the City, passed waiters sweeping the pavements outside their cafes, and asked at one for a glass of water. Eventually, at about seven, I reached Saint Peter's Basilica.

The scale of Catholicism's primary church is difficult to grasp. It is mind-bendingly big...big enough for the far reaches to have a slightly different climate or be in an adjacent time zone. Standing in the doorway and looking into the distance of the nave, I thought I glimpsed a flock of birds swooping along the horizon, just above the curly-wurly columns of Bernini's bronze canopy. Enormous though the canopy was, it looked lost in the huge void between the walls, and beneath it were the infinitesimally-tiny figures of a priest and his acolytes performing the first Mass of the day. Far, far above them, the windows around the lantern of Michelangelo's dome sent great, steady beams of early light across the mosaics. It was a breathtaking space.

Afterwards, in order to get my mind back to something resembling normal scale, I paid the entrance fee for a stroll around the Vatican corridors to see how the Pope lived. After many years of contributing to all those Sunday collections 'for the upkeep of the Holy Mother Church in Rome', it was galling to have to hand over more money at the ticket office. I felt entitled to a lifetime's free admission. But I knew, without asking, that the sour little Italian woman behind the window wouldn't agree.

Behind the mahogany double doors however, there was no 'handle on normality'. It was no one's home, but a cross between a museum and an excessive, baroque fantasy palace. Papal infallibility obviously didn't extend to restraint or taste. Gold swashes and extravagant fairground curlicues had been the decorator's stock-in-trade and the whole place, like the basilica next door, was designed to overwhelm the visitor and convey an impression of power and influence. On waxed parquet floors, glowing in the morning sunshine, stood case after inlaid case of finely-bound manuscripts. These were interspersed with gilt-framed canvases of classical mythology, portraits of Popes and Martyrs, and stunning, though often surprisingly explicit, classical sculptures. The windows were open and I was able to look down at small knots of priests having their post-breakfast perambulations on the sunlit lawns of the perfectly-tended Papal gardens.

From my stance of temporary poverty, it struck me that the Curia (despite their unenviable tendency to celibacy, and insistence on belief in The Almighty), had quite a lifestyle, but I doubted they were ever able to feel really comfortable in that mausoleum.

My pilgrimage to the seat of Catholicism didn't bring me any immediate blessings. Northwards from Rome, the lifts dried up and I spent hour-after-frustrating-hour waiting pointlessly by suburban roadsides or at the junctions of the Autostrada. Hardly anyone zooming past gave a second glance at the dusty wretch standing by the kerb. Or, if I was noticed and offered a lift, it was either going the wrong way, or just took me a few miles before turning off the main road to some village in the hills. This snail-like progress up the spine of Italy meant it took days to cover four-hundred miles and reach Milan in the north. From the road signs I stood beneath, or was occasionally driven past, I knew I was tantilisingly close to the great Renaissance towns of Florence, Sienna and Lucca. They were just down that junction or around that ring road. But I saw nothing of any of them, because I knew my sightseeing, for that journey, was over. Leonardo, Brunelleschi and Michelangelo could all wait for another day. I was tired and completely fixated on the grinding practicality, the mind-numbing slog, of getting across Europe to the Channel ports. To have turned off to gawp at those marvellous cities would have risked missing that great lift which every hitch-hiker hopes is rushing towards them in the very next car or lorry.

Anyone who thinks that time passes at a constant rate should spend a few interminable hours with their thumb extended, trying to look like potentially good company, or at least the type of passenger who won't soil the upholstery then slit the driver's throat. After all those months of travelling, I must have seemed an unprepossessing prospect – thin and bedraggled and lacking decent clothes, charm or social skills. But whatever the reason for my failure to stop a car, I knew, at this rate, and with the problems of crossing all the borders between Lombardy and the English Channel, it would take forever to get home. And there was a strong chance of what remained of my cash dribbling away at roadside food-stalls and cafés, where I occasionally needed to wolf down the cheapest thing on the menu.

It was time for a gamble.....time to finally break into Mom and Dad's folded ten pound note. I walked the few miles from the Ring Road to the main railway station in the centre of Milan and enquired about the cheapest single ticket northwards. For about £8 the clerk offered me a 'corridor pass' on a train to Paris, leaving late that night. This didn't include a seat reservation, but if I could find a place to sit, I was welcome. The cost of the fare meant that, if I cut down on everything else, especially my extravagant diet, it might just leave me enough for the Dover ferry.

The train departed just before midnight and, by ten o'clock the next day, I had left Italy, crossed the Alps, zapped through the French countryside and finally climbed down onto a platform in the Gare de Lyon.

The remainder of the journey was surprisingly easy: from Paris, two lifts took me to Calais, and, after a calm crossing with spectacular views of the white cliffs, I slept under a hedge, just north of Dover. Another thirty hours found me on an early morning No.61 bus, trundling up the Bristol Road in Brum – towards Home, Mom and Dad, Auntie Elsie and Dave, Janet, normality, and that plate of Heinz Beans on toasted white bread.

I must have cut an odd figure amongst the early morning workers in their macs, scarves and caps: I was very thin, quite sun-burned and dressed in stained and frayed cotton trousers and battered sandals held together with string. After four months of southern heat, it was nippy in that English autumn, but deep in the bowels of my rucksack I had re-discovered a thin jumper. Most of the left sleeve had unravelled and disappeared, giving it a strangely lop-sided look, but at least it provided a bit of warmth.

The conductor made his way slowly along the lower deck, and finally reached me, "Good 'oliday mate?" He asked, nodding at my battered rucksack with the dirty sleeping-bag strapped to the outside.

"Yeah....pretty good" I replied, as I sifted through my last few coins for the fare.

Appendix 1: Mike's Journey Home

Leaving the Arab sector of Jerusalem and entering Israel was like going from a poor third-world country to a rich European city. The contrast of the modern mostly-white buildings with the drab Arab style was startling. We headed straight for the port of Haifa, from where there were ferries crossing to mainland Europe, Steve and I travelling with Paul and Chris in their car. First stop was Tel Aviv and it was en route to here that Pat and Roger almost didn't make it. They were following a lorry when part of its load of heavy metal came off the back and smashed into the road just ahead of them. They were very fortunate to be able to avoid the debris flying onto the road in front of them.

We found that the most suitable ferry was to Brindisi in Italy, via Cyprus and Piraeus. The lads could not afford to ship their motorcycle or car, so sadly had to make arrangements to leave them behind with appropriate fees to the customs, much as we had to do in Ankara with our bike. There was a wait of two or three days before the ferry departed, so we camped on the beach. Another memory I have of Israel was the large number of young girls walking around with plasters over their noses, obviously just having had a "nose job".

The sea journey to Brindisi was an uneventful three days and we travelled as deck passengers. No luxury of cabins for us! Whilst we could not disembark at either Cyprus or Piraeus, we did have the marvellous experience of travelling through the Corinth Canal, a deep gash in the limestone rock, the sides of which seemed so close as though one could touch them.

We landed in Brindisi late morning faced with a fifteen-hundred-mile hitch-hike. We decided that we would travel faster singly and so in turn we waited by the side of the road for our lifts. Once we started to make our way north we lost contact with each other.

I kept to the east coast of Italy, heading for Rimini, and my first night's stop over was several miles south of there. I have no recollection of the name of the place where I stopped *or* where I spent the night. The following day passing Rimini I headed for Milan, outside of which I remember waiting a long time for a suitable lift. Part of this wait was outside a restaurant, where I remember a rather attractive girl trying, without success, to get her mother to give me a lift.

I didn't get much further that day and spent the night in my sleeping bag under a hedge to keep off the light rain. The following morning I got lucky, getting a lift with a chap going to Germany. We continued north and crossed into Switzerland via the Simplon pass, not driving through the tunnel but taking the piggy back rail system, where the cars drive on to the rolling stock, similar to the euro tunnel but without any sides or roof. I was acutely conscious of having very little money and not knowing precisely how much I would need for the ferry, and when my driver stopped at a garage for a coffee and a bite to eat I feigned I was not hungry and stayed in the car whilst he went inside. Food and drink on the way back proved to be a very minimalist affair. Passing by Basle, my Good Samaritan took me well into Germany where he dropped me off at an autobahn junction not far from the Belgium border. Again I slept in the open in a small copse by the side of the motorway and the following morning made good time with a series of lifts through Belgium and then into France, heading for the port of Dunkerque.

The following morning ferry got me into Dover. By now the big toe infection I had caught somewhere in Jordan was giving me some problems and, thoroughly fed up with hitch-hiking, I thought I would blow the rest of my money and take the train as far as London. With virtually all my money gone, my intention was to throw myself to the mercy of British Rail and offer to sign some kind of promissory note and pay for my ticket later. Needless to say this fell on deaf ears, and so, following a bus ride to the bottom of the M1, it was back on the road again. Again it had started to rain so getting a lift was difficult, however perseverance paid off and by early evening I was in Birmingham and knocking at Lois's penthouse door.

Mike Jowett - 2012

Appendix 2: Steve's Journey Home

Jerusalem to Tel Aviv, then on to Haifa.

Deck Passage to Brindisi (slept in a park and got woken by a couple of gardeners who had prepared a cup of coffee for me).

Travels through Italy: quickly learnt that worker's restaurants serve you soup in the morning as soon as you walk in, and didn't seem to mind when I ate it and left.

Rome and St Peter's – a church with no priests – they were all at lunch (with God I suppose), where I tried to get a rosary blessed for my Sister (made from the ten-millionth-part of an olive tree from the Garden of Gethsemane).

Slept in Rome's Central Station for a couple of nights then had to walk to the motorway to get a lift. Got picked up by a family who were so sorry for me they put me up for a week (can't remember the name of the town – West Coast – but enjoyed it.)

Hitched on through Italy and got a lift from a fellow who was planning to tour Switzerland, so I joined him for a couple of weeks, maybe more, and slept in the back of his van.

Got picked up by a chap who turned out to be the Minister of Science and Education in the German Bundestag. Stayed with him and his strange housekeeper for about three or four weeks in Bad Godesberg. He took me to Parliament, met Billy Brandt etc. – really interesting – and saw a lot of the Rhine Valley. Unfortunately he turned out to be gay and I had to leave quickly.

Sauntered through bits of France and eventually got a ferry from Calais to Dover – then took three or four days to get back to Five Ways and my sister's flat. She fainted when she saw me, but put me up and then took me to the family home, which had moved while I was away.

I had a threepenny piece in my pocket and swore never to do such a thing again, but now I only really remember the whole thing with affection.

Stephen Byrne - 2012

Postscript

After we dribbled back to our homes in ones and twos, were welcomed by our relieved parents, re-introduced ourselves to our girlfriends, ate the longed-for beans on toast and listened to the wonderful, newly-released 'Eleanor Rigby', I spent a lot of time reflecting on the whole adventure.

Looked at logically, it would have been easy to see our Great Mediterranean Circumnavigation Expedition as something of a failure. The journey we intended to make consisted of three 'legs' like a malformed triangle: south-east across Europe and the Balkans to Jerusalem, then west through Egypt and along Saharan North Africa. Finally, from Morocco, across the Straits of Gibraltar and north-east up through Spain and France.

But we had only completed the first leg, as far as the Holy Land, before running out of money, vehicles, commitment and energy.

And when we arrived home after four months of travel, our appearance must have been a bit of a shock for everyone who knew us, because we had all lost a lot of weight. It would have been good if we had returned leaner and fitter, but I had mislaid nearly two-and-a-half stone. Before leaving in June, I had tipped the scales at eleven stone and four pounds, but on my return, in late September, I was only eight stone nine.

Janet, my girlfriend, took a photo of me in my Sunday-best at someone's wedding soon after my return. My suit and shirt had fitted me perfectly before I left for the journey, but afterwards my weedy little neck stuck out of the collar like a baby tortoise out of his dad's shell. Sadly, when Janet and I split-up some years later, I forgot to ask for the picture.

Despite these indications of failure, the journey for me was anything but a disappointment. It had been a memorable adventure that has had an effect on the rest of my life. I had grown up a lot and gained some confidence in my ability to cope with problems (even when I had created them myself). We had seen some remarkable places at an interesting time in their history, met many good people and coped reasonably well with the few difficult ones. We had discovered that we could stray a long way from the nest and still survive (albeit whilst slowly starving), and that was a valuable lesson for an over-protected only child, who, when I was very young, wasn't allowed to play with the 'rough boys' in the Ladywood streets. And the simple joy of being somewhere unfamiliar and 'foreign' has fortunately continued (helped considerably by never having to suffer the awfulness of 'business travel' throughout my working life).

And, perhaps to the regret of the people who know me well, the experience provided me with a great fund of stories to endlessly tell and re-tell throughout the rest of my allotted span (even to the extent of writing them down).

***

Our adventures might, however, have shortened all our parent's lives. In retrospect, we must have put them through the emotional wringer, firstly before we left, as they saw our barmy preparations, then hearing, through our letters and postcards, what we were up to and how our plans were steadily degenerating, and finally when they welcomed home such a bunch of bedraggled, bony scarecrows. Now I am a father I know what it is to suffer sympathetic agonies with every problem my daughter has ever been troubled by, and therefore can now begin to grasp what all our folks went through, both before and during our absence. They must have often wondered if they'd seen the last of their sons.

My Mom and Dad had never had the opportunity, or a great desire, to visit foreign places. Their working-class, Ladywood backgrounds between the wars gave them no opportunity for distant adventures. They were grateful just to be employed. And during their courting days – when Hitler and his Third Reich were creating enough thrills to keep everyone busy – Dad was quite understandably pleased to avoid some conscripted and extremely dangerous travel. (Thanks to a suspected leaking kidney and possible diabetes, he was turned down by the Army and ordered to stay in Brum and build Lancaster bombers.) But he had always been a dreamer, and I know he understood why I wanted to go and see for myself the places he would only ever read about.

Both my folks were wonderful in their quiet determination to encourage our wanderlust and to help us in any way they could, and because we had the arrogance of young men, we believed them when they assured us that they had every confidence in our plans and abilities.

***

After Mike and Lois's Wedding in late '66, we were never all together again until their Ruby celebration forty-years-on.

I returned to being a designer with Blomberg Beaman, later became an Art School Lecturer and ended up working in the Graphics Department of the BBC. After a failed first marriage, I met Camilla and before you could say "Great Mediterranean Circumnavigation Expedition", Hattie was born. And for the following thirty years I counted myself an extremely fortunate man. We now live in Edgbaston, within a mile of Five Ways, where our journey started all those years ago. So much for wanderlust.

Our daughter is now a proper grown-up, with her own partner, house and a career as a Midwife. And these days my idea of an epic adventure is for Camilla and I to hire a car and driver and potter around bits of India – all carefully planned and with lots of helpful people to take the strain and see to the luggage.

During all those years, my fellow passengers on TOF 80 and the Matchless have rarely sat still for long:

Following his course in Building Management at Gosta Green, Michael spent his working life in the construction industry – initially in some very interesting locations: firstly the whole family spent several years in the Seychelles, where he was a Government Engineer; then after Lois and the kids returned to Bognor, he went off to work in St Petersburg and Tiblisi in Georgia, paying flying visits home to the South Coast every couple of months. When he eventually returned, he was still essentially an itinerant, spending the rest of his career travelling all over the country, helping the Home Office to build, extend and maintain Britain's prisons. He and Lois live in a roomy post-war house in Bognor Regis on a small, private estate, minutes from the sea. They have three children and a bunch of grandchildren.

I have been in touch, on-and-off, with Stephen over the years and kept a distant eye on his numerous excursions into all sorts of businesses – some successful and others that crashed in flames. The balance must have been generally in his favour, because he and his second wife, Eva, live in a stylish Georgianesque house in Chiswick. The last venture of his that I was aware of was, I think, something to do with publishing and involved 3D animations of Ancient Egyptian architecture, and the teaching of maths. He has one daughter from his first marriage and Eva also had a daughter from an earlier entanglement. I think they have at least two grandchildren, and a sea-going yacht which increasingly takes them off, over the horizon.

In 1969, three years after we all returned from our Middle Eastern wanderings, Pat and Roger bought an old Austin ambulance and set off across the world – through the Middle East, Iran, Afghanistan, Pakistan, and down into India. There, being very short of cash, they admitted that a vehicle only capable of fifteen miles to the gallon was too expensive a method of travel, and, rather than try to sell it, donated it to the nearest hospital. It had carried them all that way without a hiccup, so may well be ferrying patients around to this day.

They then continued on down through Burma and Malaysia to Singapore, and finally flew to Australia.

After working in a gold mine and helping with the upkeep of roads near Alice Springs, Pat eventually returned to Nottingham, married the girl he'd left behind, had four daughters, and now makes beautiful violins for a living. His commute to work each day is simple: just a short stroll down the garden, from their splendid Victorian house to a lavishly-equipped workshop, festooned with racks of chisels and heavy with the scent of newly-worked wood.

He told me, when we recently met up, that his tall and funny friend has never returned from Oz. Roger is living a life there, worthy of its own, very thick biography: after separating from Pat, he wandered between Australia and New Zealand, leading a complicated and tempestuous love life and being involved in two life-threatening road crashes – both times as a passenger. As a result of the second accident, he received an enormous insurance payout, and this allowed him to buy a large farm and a vineyard in Tasmania. There he now lives the life of a larger-than-life Aussie, with all the appetites, humour and boisterous explosiveness inherent in the role.

Of Chris and Paul, sadly I know nothing.

***

If life were a Hollywood film, and Al Pacino, Harrison Ford and Danny De Vito were cast as the three of us, the screenplay would open with us meeting after forty years at Mike and Lois's Ruby wedding Party in 2006. We would spend the evening daring and taunting each other into re-living our adventures on TOF 80. By the end of the evening we would have persuaded each other into buying another motorbike and setting off to tackle the whole adventure properly this time. Each would have unspoken reasons for leaving as quickly as possible: debt, business problems, blackmailing mistresses, mob double-crossings etc. But we would be full of bravado and confidence – seasoned with just a touch of desperation and neediness.

Months later, after terrible hardships, moments of touching pathos, battles with Balkan bandits, squabbles with each other, tempting encounters with exotic women, moments of self-realisation and oodles of brotherly bonding, and when everyone at home had lost hope of ever seeing us again, we would return, as better, more caring men. Waiting for us at home would be three willowy wives, dressed in chintzy Cath Kidston-style frocks, who would sense that we had changed, and had regained the qualities that had made us so attractive, all those years ago, when we first became their lovers.

Cue huge symphonic crescendo, run end-credits, not a dry eye in the house. A delightful 'Late-Life-Crisis' movie.

But in reality, I cannot imagine a sillier idea. We are now in our late-sixties, and whilst, as far as I know, still have all our original hips, knees and minds in reasonably good order (and, in the case of the other two, their hair as well), there would be a fund of pretty sticky problems to deal with before a bike was kick-started or a hankie waved in farewell:

Firstly there are the opinions of our three wives: Lois, Eva and Camilla to take into account. It would be nice to think they would miss us if we puttered off towards the horizon, but they would undoubtedly have a something to say about us absenting ourselves from our responsibilities for an indeterminate length of time. And what about the financial outpourings involved in buying the splendid Honda Goldwing and lavish equipment suitable for men who are now used to comfortable living?

Secondly, the chances of getting any form of medical cover for such a lengthy venture would be extremely doubtful – most men of our age could easily fill both sides of any insurance application form with their interesting health histories. Furthermore, I would require a fairly large compartment in the sidecar to store several months supply of my statins, soluble aspirins and hypertension pills...and added to my little stash would be whatever magical, medical potions the other two are popping every day. That would probably leave little storage space for tents and sleeping bags, let alone jerry-cans full of good Brummy water...and make us all pretty unattractive and expensive insurance risks.

Finally, the possibility of three stubborn old buggers, who have lost some of the social ease and flexibility of youth and are well set in their ways, still speaking to each other by the time we reach Dover, are very slim. It's a fair bet that at least one of us would be trying to catch a train home this side of the M25.

That epic film script might be easier to sell as a sitcom or even a farce.

***

On the wider, political stage, much of the Middle East is in turmoil and far less easy to travel through than it was in the mid-60s. What started in 2011, optimistically as 'The Arab Spring', has developed into a series of bitter and vicious internal battles:

Syria is in a state of civil war, and Bashar al-Assad is accused by most of the International Community of making war on his own citizens. This turmoil threatens to spill over into Lebanon and possibly even a border conflict with Turkey.

The Egyptians drove Hosni Mubarak into retirement and into a prison-hospital. Then, with more demonstrations in Tahrir Square, are now confronting the Military Junta that slipped quietly into his place. The newly-elected Muslim Brotherhood President is, as yet, an unknown quantity.

Libya, with the help of NATO bombs, has violently thrown off Colonel Gaddafi, but remains a troubled place, with accusations of cruel revenge, perpetrated by its disparate Militias, against suspected members of the old regime and against each other.

No one knows what the outcome of all this upheaval might be, either for the countries themselves or the world in general. If extremist Islamic movements take over the whole region, possibly under the sway of Iran, then the West has many reasons to be concerned, and Israel will be terrified for its survival, because it would be the first target for a concentrated wave of Jihadist fury.

All in all it's a bad time to revisit distant places from our past.

Perhaps that Saga coach trip to Bruges is a better bet?

Tony Fisher - September 2012

Acknowledgement

What is the most common activity undertaken whilst on a holiday? May I take a guess and suggest it may be reading?

When my colleague Dave Archer casually commented that his cousin was writing a book, I was instantly intrigued. Whilst the travel industry never provides us with a boring day in the office, an opportunity to try something new was still appealing. And the timing couldn't be better as we were just about to launch 'RB Collection', a new name to encompass all of our travel brands, and leave the door wide open for new ideas and opportunities.

On behalf of RB Collection I would like to thank Dave for bringing this idea to the table, and of course Tony for whom we have, in recent years, arranged some wonderful expeditions. None however could match up to this one, which he undertook at the age of 21, back in 1966.

We hope you enjoy reading this entertaining tale and it reminds you too of the excitement of travel.

Oliver Broad
Director, RB Collection
November 2012

About RB Collection

RB Collection is a family owned and run business based in Lichfield, Staffordshire. The collection includes the award-winning Robert Broad Travel; a community based travel agency that has attracted such accolades as Luxury Travel Agent of the Year, Central England Travel Agent of the Year and High Street Travel Agent of the Year amongst others. The collection also includes a range of specialist online travel brands such as Sports Events Travel and JordanHolidays.co.uk.

Led by Director's Oliver Broad & Nathan Collins, RB Collection's aim is to ensure their brands can develop and adapt in an ever-changing world through offering inspiring travel products.

This is RB Collection's first venture into a non-travel related product and the company looks forward to exploring other opportunities in the future.

RB Collection Ltd
2 Boley Park Shopping Centre
Lichfield
Staffs
WS14 9XU

Tel: 01543 258631

inspire@rbcollection.com
www.rbcollection.com